BECOMING A STUDENT-READY COLLEGE

BECOMING A STUDENT-READY COLLEGE

A New Culture of Leadership for Student Success

Tia Brown McNair
Susan Albertine
Michelle Asha Cooper
Nicole McDonald
Thomas Major, Jr.

Association of American Colleges and Universities

JOSSEY-BASS™
A Wiley Brand

Published by Jossey-Bass
A Wiley Brand
One Montgomery Street, Suite 1000, San Francisco, CA 94104–4594—www.josseybass.com

Jossey-Bass books and products are available through most bookstores. To contact Jossey-Bass directly call our Customer Care Department within the U.S. at 800–956–7739, outside the U.S. at 317–572–3986, or fax 317–572–4002.

Wiley publishes in a variety of print and electronic formats and by print-on-demand. Some material included with standard print versions of this book may not be included in e-books or in print-on-demand. If this book refers to media such as a CD or DVD that is not included in the version you purchased, you may download this material at http://booksupport.wiley.com. For more information about Wiley products, visit www.wiley.com.

Library of Congress Cataloging-in-Publication Data is Available

9781119119517 (Hardcover)
9781119119524 (ePub)
9781119119531 (ePDF)

Cover image: © Nanisimova/iStockphoto
Cover design: Wiley

Printed in the United States of America

FIRST EDITION
HB Printing   SKY10028108_071221

For Maurice and Austin, and for my parents, William and Patricia, and sister Tammi. Thank you for always supporting me. —TBM

For Vera, who in the 1950s taught me to see, and for all my students. —SA

For the Cooper family and all the relatives and friends who have supported me on this journey. —MAC

For Dr. Stacy C. Boyd for his prayers, encouragement, and support, and to Dr. Harold L. Nixon for the legacy you established in me. —NM

For Linda, Eric, and Rachael, with all my love. —TM

Joint dedication: *For all of America's college students—previous, current, and future. This book is for you and your success!*

CONTENTS

PREFACE

"Students today are not prepared for postsecondary education"

"Why are we admitting students who are not ready for college?"

"Are we lowering our academic standards?"

"Students are not motivated. It is not my responsibility to convince them that getting an education is important for their lifelong success."

"I am too busy to mentor students."

"It is their responsibility to learn how to navigate college. I did it. Why can't they?"

If any of these statements sound familiar to you—whether it was heard in a meeting or in a conversation with colleagues, or you have thought them—then this book is for you. First, we want to be clear that this book is not about judgment or casting blame. We embarked on this journey because we believe in the promise and vision of higher education, but we also recognize the constraints and the frustration of our colleagues, and even ourselves, in trying to do the work we are committed to accomplishing. This book is our effort to reframe the dialogue on student success. To create a paradigm shift, from focusing more on what students lack to focusing more on what we can do, as educators, to create stronger, higher-quality educational environments that promote full inclusion and continuous improvement.

The central theme for this book emerged from a conversation at a meeting in Indianapolis. A couple of us were talking about how institutions can examine their institutional efforts to improve student success. Not surprisingly, the conversation shifted to some form of the quotes just listed. Instead of going down a path of blaming the students, Thomas asked a very provocative question: "We talk a lot about students not being college-ready, but why don't we ask what it means to be a student-ready college?" From that one question, the concept for this book was born.

Our goal is for this book to be a catalyst for action and for change at postsecondary institutions. To accomplish this goal, the book should be a discussion driver. We have included a series of principles, case examples, and questions to prompt discussions. We hope that the book encourages institutional assessment and self-reflection.

ABOUT THE AUTHORS

Tia Brown McNair, Ed.D., has spent the past 20 years advocating for underserved students in higher education through various administrator roles and as an adjunct faculty member at several institutions. She currently is the vice president of Diversity, Equity, and Student Success at the Association of American Colleges and Universities (AAC&U), where she leads national efforts to improve quality in undergraduate education by Making Excellence Inclusive. She oversees both funded projects and AAC&U's continuing programs on equity, diversity, inclusive excellence, high-impact educational practices, and student success. McNair also directs AAC&U's Summer Institute on High-Impact Educational Practices and Student Success.

Susan Albertine, Ph.D., University of Chicago, began teaching middle school in 1971. She later became a professor of English and served in an array of academic leadership positions, including vice provost for undergraduate studies, Temple University, and dean of humanities and social sciences, The College of New Jersey. In 2008 she joined the Association of American Colleges and Universities; she was promoted to vice president, Office of Diversity, Equity, and Student Success, through 2015, when she became Senior Scholar for Faculty.

Michelle Asha Cooper, Ph.D., is the president of the Institute for Higher Education Policy (IHEP)—one of the nation's most effective voices in championing access and success for all students in postsecondary education. With a career rooted in the postsecondary community, Cooper has held various leadership positions at the Advisory Committee on Student Financial Assistance (Advisory Committee) at the U.S. Department of Education, Association of American Colleges and Universities, Council for Independent Colleges, and King's College. An expert on various higher education issues, Cooper is well versed in higher education access and success (domestic and international), with special emphasis on equitable reform of higher education, financial aid simplification and policy, student success outcomes, institutional accountability, diversity and equity, and other national higher education trends and policies.

Nicole McDonald, Ph.D., works as a strategy officer at Lumina Foundation, the nation's largest private foundation committed solely to increasing higher education attainment in the United States, and is responsible for developing strategic approaches to increase the educational attainment of college students. Her portfolio includes initiatives to help institutions increase student success and develop high-quality credentials and pathways. Previously, she served as the system director for transfer and retention with the Kentucky Community and Technical College System (KCTCS). Her background includes education policy as well as academic and student affairs administration—including work as an associate in academic affairs at the Kentucky Council on Postsecondary Education, and work in various capacities at Vanderbilt and

Emory Universities, and the Tennessee Higher Education Commission.

Thomas Major, Jr., J.D., serves as corporate counsel at Lumina Foundation. Thomas develops and implements strategies to advance Goal 2025—increasing the percentage of Americans who hold high-quality degrees and credentials to 60 percent by the year 2025. In addition to supporting Lumina's general counsel on a wide variety of legal and fiduciary matters, Thomas' work focuses on supporting efforts that engage higher education systems and institutions to increase completion rates and close attainment gaps of historically underrepresented and low-income students. Thomas' professional background includes private corporate law practice, educational consulting, and various roles in workforce development.

ABOUT AAC&U

AC&U is the leading national association concerned with the quality, vitality, and public standing of undergraduate liberal education. Its members are committed to extending the advantages of a liberal education to all students, regardless of academic specialization or intended career. Founded in 1915, AAC&U now comprises more than 1,300 member institutions—including accredited public and private colleges, community colleges, research universities, and comprehensive universities of every type and size.

AAC&U functions as a catalyst and facilitator, forging links among presidents, administrators, and faculty members who are engaged in institutional and curricular planning. Its mission is to reinforce the collective commitment to liberal education and inclusive excellence at both the national and local levels, and to help individual institutions keep the quality of student learning at the core of their work as they evolve to meet new economic and social challenges.

Information about AAC&U membership, programs, and publications can be found at www.aacu.org.

ACKNOWLEDGMENTS

Throughout this process, we have had the support of family, friends, and colleagues; they are too many to name, but all are deeply appreciated, so with sincere gratitude we say thank you. We especially want to thank Christina Duhig, program associate in the Office of Diversity, Equity and Student Success at the Association of American Colleges and Universities (AAC&U) and Kathryn Peltier Campbell, editor, Diversity & Democracy, and coordinating editor for Gender Equity in Education, Office of Communications, Policy and Public Engagement, AAC&U. Christina spent countless hours including references, reviewing chapters, and organizing files for submissions. Kathryn reviewed and offered extensive feedback on the first draft. Her insights and recommendations helped shape the structure of the book. We are indebted to both of them for their time, commitment, and encouragement.

A special thank-you to our editor, Marjorie McAneny, for her patience and support throughout this process.

Finally, we hope you find the book useful in your discussions and, more important, we hope that the book is a catalyst for the needed change that is embedded in the hope and promise of higher education for all students. The action that we seek to inspire is practical, but not easy. Our inspiration comes from the level of enthusiasm we encounter from colleagues during our professional journeys, even in the midst of frustration, limited resources, and diminished time and capacity. We hope that your reason for choosing this book is because you, too, want to lead a paradigm shift from focusing solely on college-ready students to exploring what it means to become a student-ready institution and the action required to achieve this goal.

CHAPTER·ONE

In Search of the Student-Ready College

In higher education, college administrators and faculty often talk about their desire to identify better and more college-ready students. They want students who come to college ready to learn and ready for the rigors of postsecondary education. On the surface, having college-ready students is a worthy goal. However, this assumes that most students are not ready to handle the rigors of postsecondary education. In actuality, that's not completely true. Most students aspire to college, and many have taken steps to prepare for college. While it is true that a sizable percentage of today's college students struggle academically, even then, these students should have viable postsecondary options available to them. In this search for the college-ready student, we put the burden of readiness and preparation on the student, when in reality, preparing today's students for the rigors of college should be a shared responsibility. Just imagine if we focused on the other side of that coin, and instead of seeking the ideal student, we became the ideal college. The college that was prepared for today's students, regardless of their backgrounds and academic strengths and challenges. What if we became a student-ready college? Interesting concept, isn't it?

But what does that really mean? What does it mean to be a student-ready college? Being a student-ready college requires more than a mission or diversity statement that touts philosophical ideals of inclusiveness. Being a student-ready college even means more than expressed commitments to inclusion and student-centeredness. A student-ready college is one that strategically and holistically advances student success, and works tirelessly to educate *all* students for civic and economic participation in a global, interconnected society.

At student-ready colleges, all services and activities—from admissions, to the business office, to the classroom, and even to campus security—are intentionally designed to facilitate students' progressive advancement toward college completion and positive post-college outcomes. Student-ready colleges are committed not only to student achievement, but also to organizational learning and institutional improvement. At student-ready colleges, all principles and values are aligned with the mission of the institution, and those beliefs are shared among members of the broader campus community. Student-ready colleges offer a holistic approach to leadership that empowers all members of the campus community to serve as leaders and educators.

In this book, we will explore the ecosystem of the student-ready college. We intend to think systemically and to offer an organic model based on ideas and practices we have learned from our years of work with campuses. College campuses often function as an ecosystem. Sometimes it is in good health; sometimes it is not so healthy, but in need of nurturing and change. Growth always occurs one way or another. And the campus ecosystem doesn't exist in isolation. Campuses are part of the web or network of life in a community. Surrounded by and interconnected with other organizations and social structures, businesses and civic bodies, the campus participates in the life of the community. At the state and national level, the campus is interconnected systemically in a host of ways. Funding, regulations, laws, business practices, health and wellness functions, and the daily stuff of life—food, water, housing, transportation—all connect the campus to its broader community, its state, and the nation. When we think about the meaning and practice of leadership of the student-ready college, it is this environmental and organic meaning that we emphasize.

This book is written by five deeply committed leaders from the higher education community. Through our collective experience and wisdom, we have served higher education in a variety of leadership positions, within academic institutions and alongside them. We have worked with policy and philanthropic leaders who seek to advance and support efforts aligned with increased college attainment. Our commitment to today's students—and the institutions that serve them well—are reflected in our recommendations.

Through this collaboration, we endeavor to highlight the most promising and innovative practices we have witnessed across the community. Although the strategies outlined in this book can be undertaken by individual leaders alone, we recommend a collective approach—bringing together administrators and faculty across the college community to mobilize these efforts. Additionally, we suggest steps for partnering with those outside the campus community, as sustained progress will require partnerships—both internal and external—that can engage in a concerted, sustained effort.

The examples we offer are not exhaustive, but they reflect a range of interventions occurring all across the postsecondary community. But even with these enterprising models and initiatives, there is still a dearth of resources for institutional leaders to draw from. We hope this book adds to the collection of tools and resources that faculty, administrators, policy and philanthropic leaders, and all those who care about today' college students can draw upon for practical solutions.

A New Concept: Student-Ready Colleges

The goal of becoming a student-ready college is not difficult to embrace for most educators. In fact, if this concept were more prevalent, we believe that more people would readily embrace it. After all, supporting students is an aspiration of all campus leaders. Although we suspect that many will resonate with this concept, we also recognize that, for some, enacting our recommendations may pose a challenge. The problem is not really a lack of will; rather, some colleges are simply not structured to support this level of engagement; for others, there is no expectation or requirement to be student-centric; and there are still others who struggle with competing pressures and demands. When faced with these factors, some institutional leaders—even those sensitive to student needs and diversity—may fall back on old subconscious habits, which expect students to conform to traditional norms and standards. This approach often hurts students, as it leads to feelings of isolation and disconnection, the precursors to poor performance and outcomes. Also, this approach perpetuates the status quo—and in the 21st century, the status quo is no longer an option.

The impetus for writing this book is a growing awareness that the realities confronting our higher education system have the potential to narrow and threaten opportunity for millions of today's students. Therefore, we desire to work alongside campus leaders and faculty to minimize these threats. As was the case for previous generations of college-goers, the issues of college accessibility, affordability, and preparation remain, but they are further complicated by demographic, economic, and technological changes that are altering how we think, learn, and work. Beyond these compounding factors, we already know that the current educational system does not support existing students well. If left unchecked, these convergent forces could have catastrophic effects on our 21st-century students. We need these students. We need them to succeed. So it is critical that we transform our institutional culture and practices to be student-ready—responsive to contemporary students' needs and realities.

For many institutional leaders, this change will require more than tweaks or marginal changes; rather, it will require an overhaul of institutional policies and practices, as well as individual and shared attitudes and values. To enable and support institutional leaders committed to being student-ready institutions, we offer this practical, action-oriented book.

The Quest for College-Ready Students: A Historical Perspective

Although our goal should be to create student-ready colleges, sometimes we fail to tackle the institutional bureaucracies and deficits hindering progress toward this goal, but opt for a different strategy. This alternative approach removes the onus for improvement from the institution—or other structural impediments—and places it squarely on the student. In this strategy, we focus our energy on searching for the ideal college student—the "college-ready student." The vision of this college-ready student can take on a range of forms, with high-achieving, self-directed students on one end and students with high potential on the other. Regardless of where we place our vision of the ideal student along this spectrum, there is a belief among many within the higher education community that there simply are not enough of them. As a result, faculty and administrators sometimes lament the challenges of educating today's students and are nostalgic for a prior era in American higher education when the students were (seemingly) different.

Although admittedly there are differences between the students of today and previous cohorts, their similarities are fundamental. Like prior generations of students, today's students arrive at college with a desire to learn and grow both personally and professionally. Regardless of the decade in which they enter college, students believe that a college degree is a prerequisite for a good life. Students have always believed that participating and succeeding in higher education will allow them to tap into greater levels of self-awareness and capability. They also share in the expectation that college will prepare them to live and make a living. Hence, for generations, students have arrived at the doorsteps of our colleges and universities with high expectations and varying academic and personal needs. And historically, our colleges and universities have responded accordingly, seizing the opportunity to nurture and prepare these students to lead meaningful, productive lives.

Over the years, higher education has always aimed to be responsive to the concerns of its students, but the present day finds too many of us either solemn in our quest to find the ideal college student or too constrained by external forces and demands to think outside of the box. Given this, we long for and reminisce about a golden age in American higher education, when students all came to college well prepared and resources were readily available to support them. But this never was the case; the idea that an ideal student or ideal college existed "once upon a time" is nothing more than a myth. America's colleges and universities have always appealed to students with diverse interests and levels of academic preparation, and resources have always had to be negotiated. The challenge for us today is that our system of higher education has grown exponentially over the last three centuries—and growth continues. As it grows, so do the numbers of students who need additional support and preparation.

Clark Kerr wrote, "an appreciation of the evolution of higher education helps to develop perspective on contemporary issues, since historical context often reveals that our present problems are not all new ones" (as cited in Bullard, 2007, p. 12). In other words, the realities faced by today's college students simply provide a contemporary spin on issues encountered previously. A quick review of the history of higher education reveals that changing student needs have always stretched the system; and the system has, in turn, always adapted to accommodate the realities of the emergent student population. Even going back to the founding of the nation's first colleges in the seventeenth and eighteenth centuries—when going to college was a rarity except for those interested in the clergy—we find that Harvard College provided tutors in Greek and Latin for those underprepared students (Institute for Higher Education Policy, 1998).

During the 19th century, higher education witnessed one of its most significant shifts with the passage of the Morrill Land-Grant Acts (i.e., the Morrill Act of 1862 and the Morrill Act of 1890). The Morrill Acts gave birth to public postsecondary education and expanded opportunity to thousands of Americans who previously would not have had access to college. With the establishment of these colleges to teach agricultural and mechanical courses, institutions found it necessary to offer preparatory programs for students struggling in reading, writing, and mathematics.

Similar to the expansion witnessed by the Morrill Act of 1862, the Morrill Act of 1890 was the nation's first attempt to ensure college access to all Americans, not just White Americans, as it designated separate land-grant institutions for persons of color and gave birth to today's historically Black colleges and universities (Thelin, 2011; Gasman, 2008). This student growth was accompanied by an increase in the need for additional student supports. In 1894, with a college student enrollment of approximately 238,000, more than 40 percent of college freshmen enrolled in precollegiate programs (Ignash, 1997). Even at elite institutions, such as Harvard, Princeton, and Yale, sizeable proportions of the student body struggled academically and required additional supports from the institution to ensure their success.

The Morrill Acts introduced the first wave of growth and accessibility in higher education, and the second wave was the result of the GI Bill in 1944. This legislation spawned massive growth in the postsecondary system, making college more accessible and affordable. The GI Bill is popularly thought to have changed the face of America as well as the face of our nation's colleges and universities (Thelin, 2011). Throughout the 20th century, other seminal legislative efforts—including the Civil Rights Act of 1965 and the Higher Education Act of 1965—helped to make higher education more accessible and affordable for millions more Americans (Thelin, 2011). As a result of these policies, thousands of deserving students enrolled in college, and while many had to adjust to the social dimensions of higher education, several faced academic challenges as well.

The current era of higher education—in the opening decades of the 21st century—presents another watershed moment in our nation's history. As we grapple with daunting realities—stemming from the social, demographic, technological, and economic changes impacting higher education—attaining a postsecondary degree or credential is becoming even more important to support career development and social mobility. To ensure that higher education works well for all students, the system needs to adapt to student needs and realities. There has never been a time when all students enrolled in college were academically prepared, when no students required additional supports to promote their college success, or when the transition from high school to college was seamless for all students. In our present-day quest for the ideal student, we miss opportunities to transform our institutions and teaching practices in support of today's students. Instead, too many of us are beginning to absolve ourselves from responsibility associated with poor student outcomes. We place the blame on either the individual student, the K–12 system, or broader societal challenges, such as poverty.

While inequality and disparities in society and the K–12 system do contribute to postsecondary challenges, higher education also plays a role in creating and perpetuating systemic barriers that impede student progress and success. For example, higher education leaders rarely acknowledge how higher education's expectations, practices, policies, and unspoken rules further stratify and marginalize students. To better support current and future generations of students, higher education must undergo a paradigm shift—one in which faculty and administrators fully embrace responsibility for serving students. History has shown that navigating such change is possible.

A Profile of the 21st-Century Student

To strengthen our democracy, colleges and universities must offer students a high-quality educational experience that teaches them "how to work" and "how to live" in this 21st-century knowledge economy (Wagner, 2010). For centuries, the U.S. system of higher education has been a leader in postsecondary education, boasting some of the strongest outcomes and institutions in the world. U.S. institutions are recognized in worldwide rankings of colleges and universities, holding more than half of the top 100 spots as well as 8 of the top 10. Many world leaders in the sciences and humanities are graduates of U.S. colleges and universities.

Even for those who do not achieve these levels of success, the benefits correlated with earning a college degree have been documented (Baum, Ma, & Payea, 2013). For example:

- Higher educational levels reduce the chances of being unemployed:

    "The 2012 unemployment rates for 25- to 34-year-olds were 9.6% for those with some college but no degree and 7.2% for those with associate degrees" (p. 20).

- Attaining a college degree increases the likelihood of moving up the socioeconomic ladder:

    "Of adults who grew up in the middle family income quintile, 31% of those with a four-year college degree moved up to the top income quintile between 2000 and 2008, compared with just 12% of those without a four-year college degree" (p. 22).

- Adults with a college education exhibit higher levels of civic engagement:

  "In 2012, 42% of four-year college graduates, 29% of adults with some college or an associate degree, and 17% of high school graduates volunteered for organizations" (p. 5).

Even as the value proposition for higher education remains high, student success outcomes and graduation rates are uneven and below average. There are currently more than 20 million students enrolled in over 6,000 postsecondary institutions (National Center for Education Statistics, 2014), but only 4 out of 10 Americans hold a college degree or credential (U.S. Census Bureau, 2014). Another 25 percent attempted college, but left without a degree (Lumina Foundation, 2015c). We also know that these subpar outcomes disproportionately impact students from traditionally underserved racial/ethnic groups, who represent growing sectors of higher education—fewer than 30 percent of Blacks (28), Hispanics (20), and Native Americans (24) between the ages of 25 and 64 have earned a college degree (see Figure 1.1). And a recent examination of millennials shows that the career readiness among recent graduates is unsatisfactory, with deficits in skills associated with literacy, math, and problem solving (Goodman, Sands, & Coley, 2015).

With the face of American higher education changing, it is imperative that we embrace new models of education and support services that can accommodate today's college students.

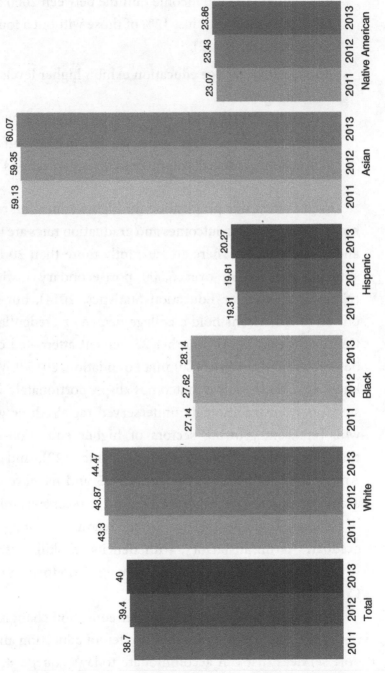

Figure 1.1   Trends in Degree Attainment Rates for U.S. Residents

Percentage by Population Group (Ages 25–64).

Source: Lumina Foundation, 2015c.

To serve these students, we must first have a precise under-standing of the profile for 21st-century college students. At present, students of color compose more than 40 percent of the student body, and that proportion is expected to increase, with the growth being fueled by Latino/a and Asian students. And over 70 percent of today's college students possess nontradi-tional or post-traditional student characteristics (Miller, Valle, Engle, & Cooper, 2014), with 44 percent being over the age of 24 and over 25 percent enrolling part-time (30 percent), having dependents (28 percent), or working full-time (26 percent). In addition, growing proportions of these students are from first-generation (52 percent), low-income (51 percent), minor-ity (42 percent), and non-native English speaking (18 percent) backgrounds (Figure 1.2). Also, as the civil rights of those of diverse sexual orientations are advanced nationally, we expect to serve even more students who reflect the lesbian, gay, bisexual, and transgender (LGBT) communities (Pew Research Center, 2013).

Historical trends show that there has been steady enroll-ment growth among diverse student groups—with these post-traditional characteristics—for decades. But the trends in accessibility have not translated into better student outcomes. In fact, college completion rates for many underserved student groups continue to lag far behind national averages.

- Part-time students, for example, rarely graduate. Even when these students take twice as long to complete degrees or certificates, no more than a quarter ever make it to grad-uation day (Complete College America, 2014).

Figure 1.2   Profile of Today's Student

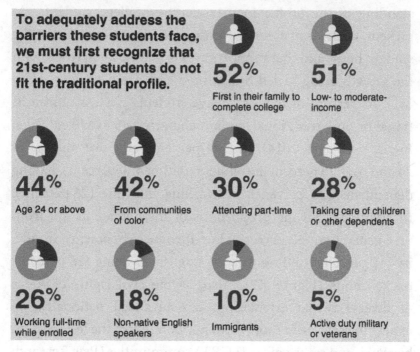

To adequately address the barriers these students face, we must first recognize that 21st-century students do not fit the traditional profile.

52% First in their family to complete college

51% Low- to moderate-income

44% Age 24 or above

42% From communities of color

30% Attending part-time

28% Taking care of children or other dependents

26% Working full-time while enrolled

18% Non-native English speakers

10% Immigrants

5% Active duty military or veterans

Source: Miller, Valle, Engle, & Cooper, 2014.

- Minority students still struggle to graduate—less than 30 percent of African Americans (28 percent), Native Americans (23 percent), and Latinos/as (20 percent) complete college (Lumina Foundation, 2015c [Figure 1.3]).

- Low-income students are only half as likely as their higher-income peers to earn a bachelor's degree, even though attaining this degree substantially increases their chances of moving out of poverty (Lumina Foundation, 2015c [Figure 1.3]). If low-income young adults earned bachelor's degrees at the same rate as their higher-income counterparts, the United States would rank even higher among the top developed countries in the world.

Figure 1.3   Attainment Rate for Low-Income Students

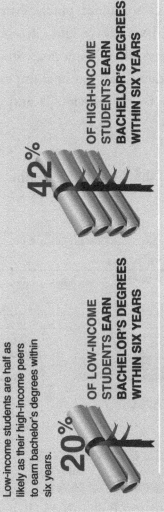

Low-income students are half as likely as their high-income peers to earn bachelor's degrees within six years.

20% OF LOW-INCOME STUDENTS EARN BACHELOR'S DEGREES WITHIN SIX YEARS

42% OF HIGH-INCOME STUDENTS EARN BACHELOR'S DEGREES WITHIN SIX YEARS

Low-income individuals are five times more likely to move out of poverty if they attain a college degree.

5X LOW-INCOME INDIVIDUALS ARE MORE LIKELY TO MOVE OUT OF POVERTY IF THEY ATTAIN A COLLEGE DEGREE

Source: Miller, Valle, Engle, & Cooper, 2014.

These facts show that the American system of higher education simply does not work well for everyone, and far too many students encounter challenges all along the educational pipeline that lead to the end of their formal education (see Figures 1.3 and 1.4). These trends are unacceptable, especially at a time when a more educated workforce and citizenry are so desperately needed. Educating all of America's students, especially underrepresented students, is a national imperative, as it can lead to positive impacts for individuals and entire communities.

Figure 1.4 The Reality of the Education Pipeline

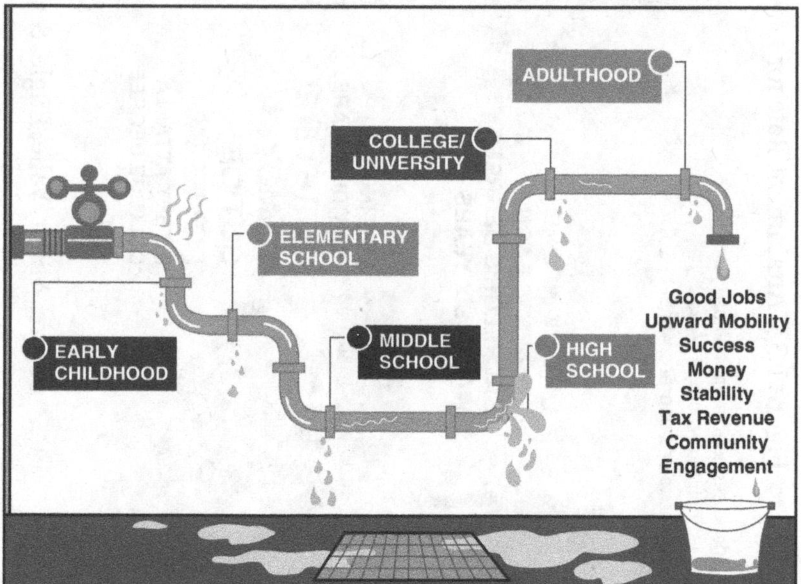

Source: Institute for Higher Education Policy, 2013 (Reprinted from Literacy Connects).

Serving Students? Responding to Markets? Competing Tensions in Higher Education

Throughout the history of higher education, the community has responded to significant changes to the landscape; however, these responses have not consistently been student-driven or student-centric. Often, the community's response has been led by an economic-based or market-driven approach, known as academic capitalism (Giroux, 2014; Manning, 2013; Park, 2012; Andrews, 2006; Slaughter & Leslie, 1997). Academic capitalism refers to the "market and market-like behaviors on the part of universities and faculty" (Slaughter & Leslie, 1997, p. 11) to gain additional resources and, sometimes, even prestige.

The economic factors occurring outside of the academy make the shift toward academic capitalism feel inevitable for higher education. With the decline in state government support, for example, academic capitalism is used to justify transforming academic and nonacademic functions into profit-making ventures. Academic capitalism manifests in different ways and can vary within and across campuses. But most commonly, it leads to the development of alternative income streams (i.e., competitive research grants, training, rental of facilities), outsourcing (i.e., of bookstores, contingent faculty labor, dining services, and health care), and diversification of academic programs (i.e., online and distance education; Slaughter & Rhoades, 2009; Volk, Slaughter & Thomas, 2001).

Although discussed as a fairly new concept within the field of higher education, permutations of academic capitalism have always been present. Non-profit universities, in fact, have always engaged in for-profit activities, most notably through athletics and campus bookstores. But now, this phenomenon is spreading and quickly becoming the "new normal." Institutional priorities are being shaped using this concept more readily, as campus leaders find that their decision making is being influenced—implicitly and explicitly—by the tenets of academic capitalism.

As academic capitalism becomes more influential in the higher education enterprise, more people are becoming acutely aware of the opportunities and limitations of this approach, as it has the potential to be both helpful and harmful. Given this, it is important to ensure that this approach is not detrimental to the institutional ethos and does not compromise key components, such as teaching and learning. It is also necessary to ensure that this market-influenced approach has no adverse effects on underserved students. As a result, higher education leaders must not allow corporate functions and market forces to "reign supreme over the fundamental tenets of higher education" (Giroux, 2014; Manning, 2013; Andrews, 2006; Slaughter & Leslie, 1997); instead, the need for short-term profitability must be balanced with long-term investments in students and learning.

Even with a more conscientious approach to academic capitalism, some argue that market concepts are simply incongruent with the core functions of higher education and will ultimately prove detrimental to academic freedom and teaching, thereby compromising student outcomes and success. In *Lowering Higher Education: The Rise of Corporate Universities and the Fall of Liberal Education* (2011), Côte and Allahar argue that these market approaches have commodified education and learning. "Students have become consumers, colleges have turned into vendors, and research is being commercialized in applied fields marking a new era in higher education as an entrepreneurial institution" (Chait as cited in Bullard, 2007, p. 2).

On the other hand, some higher education leaders believe that market-centric approaches can be complementary to student-centric approaches. When approached with this perspective, student success and academic principles serve as the foundation for institutional culture and leadership; then academic capitalism becomes a tool or strategy that drives resource generation, leads to opportunities for faculty collaboration and development, leverages institutional partnerships, and, most important, creates pathways and support structures that benefit students. The synergy derived from having these two concepts operate in concert, instead of at odds, actually aids the quest for the ideal student, because it transforms the institution into a student-centric or student-ready college, where ideal college students are nurtured and developed.

Becoming more student-ready or student-centric can lead to tremendous market advantages, but only when institutional leaders make it a priority to know, understand, and respond to the needs of their students. When institutional leaders understand the similarities and unique qualities of 21st-century students, in comparison to students from previous generations, they can take steps to deliberately align institutional strategies in support of them. In reality, the most responsible market solution for achieving long-term financial and learning outcomes is to be a student-ready college.

The Path Forward: Taking Steps to Transformation

Policymakers and the general public habitually criticize American higher education. One could make the point that as long as higher education has existed in the United States, people have always been critical. Criticism extends from educators and their policies and practices to the impact of education, or lack thereof, on students. Certainly there are elements of truth in some of the criticism, but there are ways to address these critiques and improve the higher education system. In this book, we are turning away from criticism and thinking about improvement as growth and progression. We intend to offer a useful corrective, but we do so from a positive vantage point that offers new questions and opens new perspectives on what it means to create a student-ready campus.

This book is written for all campus educators, but it is intended to spur action primarily among campus leadership and decision makers. We hope that readers will take from this book a set of principled recommendations that will offer a framework for aligning attitudes and behavior with the steps needed for success. Acknowledging that we are making the case for cultural and organizational change, we speak with humility. We know this work is hard, and it takes bravery and passion to even consider what we recommend. But through our work, we have encountered many courageous men and women ready to tackle the challenges, but unaware of where or how to start. We believe that the best time to start is now, and the best place to start is where you are as you turn the pages of this book.

CHAPTER·TWO

Leadership Values and Organizational Culture

Guiding Questions

- How can campus values support an effort to make the campus ready for students?

- How can campus leaders engage the whole community and governance in this effort?

- How can campus leaders make a case for change based on an urgent, shared, and powerful vision?

Perspective Taking

L et's start with the premise that all campus communities embrace their own core values. Some observers believe that these values or value systems set higher education apart from corporate culture (Kezar & Lester, 2009). We might conclude that while all campus values are significant, some carry more potential to do well than others. In this chapter we invite you to consider your perspective on leadership and to pay attention to your values and the values held by your campus community. We hope that you will do two things. First, we suggest you take a close look at your own values in the context of your campus's values. Then we hope you will experiment with some perspective taking on your position as a campus leader. What might happen if you were to use the concept of the student-ready campus as a source of values you can hold and serve? What if, as a result, you upended or reversed your thinking about whatever job you do on your campus? How might that help you to do things that contribute to the value system held by your campus and to the way values are enacted within campus governance?

A Casual Conversation with a Community College President from the Mid-Atlantic Region, Summer 2015

"A book on making colleges ready for students? That's a great idea. We are doing that sort of work in so many ways. We consider everybody who works on the campus to be an educator. We say it in our convocations, and we mean it! Everyone carries that responsibility because we care as a community about our students. We even have advising guidelines for staff to help them make the most of opportunities to be mentors."

"That's excellent. Are those guidelines available publicly? I would love to cite them."

"I'm not certain. We'll have to look."

Observation: The will is there, and leaders are just beginning to find the way.

To begin: an exercise in perspective taking can be illuminating. Ask any seasoned composition instructor what she does to help students who have trouble writing unlock their creativity and bust through writer's block. You will hear, time and again, that the way to unlock and unblock is to alter perspective. The same basic advice serves for student-ready leadership. One can find a new vantage point on leadership for a student-ready campus and find renewal and creativity in leadership that serves the values of that vision. You as an individual leader may hold this value, but what in fact can you point to as having been done to achieve it? Being ready for students has to be more than aspirational. You have to share the vision.

New Directions for Leadership

- What would it mean for you to be a student-ready leader?

- What would you do that is different?

We invite you to consider a new perspective as you reflect on and explore essential responsibilities, structures, and recommendations for leadership for a student-ready campus. The recommendations of this chapter flow from the belief in students that animates this book. We have introduced the concept of a belief in students in the opening chapter and will explore that belief more fully in chapter five, "Demonstrating Belief in Students." This chapter addresses values held by a community of educators and the structures and functions of campus governance—specifically shared governance—in relation to campus values. We are taking a principled position that just as all students have the capacity to learn, all people who work on campus have the capacity to be effective educators and leaders. Similarly, the shared governance structures we build, creaky and problematic as they may sometimes be, actually can accomplish a great deal of good. We have the capacity collectively in higher education in the United States to work more effectively with the students we have and the students we will have.

In some respects, the beliefs and matters of principle presented in this chapter are commonsensical and noncontroversial. But from some angles, as we will see, they might be provocative. As we develop further in chapters three and four, we are taking a holistic approach to the campus as an ecosystem and working with principles and concepts of distributed and developmental leadership for a healthy and flourishing organizational culture. We are looking for something closer to what Kucia and Gravett (2014) call "leaders in balance" rather than "leaders in control" (Kezar, 2015, p. 21; Schroeder, 2010).

A Short Clipping from the *Chronicle of Higher Education*, March 9, 2015

Leading Beyond the Hierarchy

In *Leadership in Balance: New Habits of the Mind* (2014), John F. Kucia and Linda S. Gravett argue that "leaders in balance" can often be more effective than "leaders in control." That's especially true for today's higher-education environment, in which thinking beyond the hierarchy is increasingly prized as a technique for fostering creativity, says Mr. Kucia, administrative vice president at Xavier University.

A leader in balance, the authors say, embodies these traits:

- Approaches leadership as a relationship, not a position.

- Understands that the leader embodies the promise of the brand.

- Is motivated by a higher purpose; believes that mission drives the numbers.

- Acknowledges that collaboration must have a business purpose.

- Thinks "outside the pyramid" in order to share power and to spread leadership, authority, and responsibility.

- Believes that teaching and leadership have much in common.

- Understands that a personal comfort with diversity is at the center of collaboration.

More, however, than issuing an invitation to practice shared and distributed leadership, we intend to illustrate an intentional top-down and bottom-up, inside-out and outside-in approach to leadership that is specifically inclusive of all campus con-stituencies. Emphasizing the roles and responsibilities of administrators, faculty, and staff, we want to address educators' roles and rewards and community stewardship. The changing nature of faculty work and the changing characteristics of educators figure into this inclusive approach. To create a student-ready campus, the campus community will need to embrace a vision of student-ready leadership and then act on that vision. It will need to imagine and support action in service of this vision—and do this work in a highly intentional and inclusive way. Starting now. Starting where people are right now, wherever that may be. While few campuses have made changes to leadership as comprehensive as envisioned here, many campuses have been moving in this direction. It is possible to point to key practices and actions that student-ready leaders can use, no matter where they are beginning.

We have written this chapter with senior administrators in mind, but we hope that our recommendations will be useful to any educator on a campus. An ecological and distributed model of leadership acknowledges traditional hierarchies of responsibility and authority while being open and welcoming to all. We believe in working with the people and structures we have, recognizing that they can change through more purposeful collaboration. We are taking a searching look at orthodoxies, or closely held beliefs, related to leadership and envisioning how they may be flipped or reversed (Nagji and Walters, 2011, pp. 60–65) to help us change perspective.

A holistic plan for student-ready leadership will need to proceed from a new mindset or set of attitudes. To make your campus ready for students, you will need to work with principles—likely new principles—that are aligned with the mission and values of the campus and shared among campus community members. We urge you to consider multifaceted leadership activity as a resource to be used intentionally across the institution. This kind of leadership is open and welcoming to all educators, for the benefit of all students. Accordingly, we offer two approaches to leadership, each addressing a key principle.

Changing Perspective on Educators

Principle One: All people who work on campus have the capacity to be effective educators.

- How can a student-ready campus empower leadership where it may not yet exist?

- Is it possible to take a holistic approach based on a belief that everyone who works on the campus can be an educator and a leader?
- What would it mean to take such a principle seriously?
- What would then have to change?

As we have just suggested, we invite you to think and act as if the campus as a whole has a stake in leadership, with the senior administration standing firmly in support of this model. In management literature, distributed leadership practices, for example, often take a whole system approach. We recommend such approaches to leaders who want to find new means and models for collaboration. A wealth of good guidance is also available in Adrianna Kezar and Jaime Lester's *Organizing Higher Education for Collaboration: A Guide for Campus Leaders* (2009). Especially valuable are their observations on social networking and power dynamics:

> Perhaps the greatest challenge is for campuses that do not have any values similar to student centeredness, innovation, egalitarianism, capacity building, or efficiency that appeal to collaboration. This is a very real challenge; manifesting new values on a campus is a very complex process that often takes years to develop. (p. 96)

Does Collaboration Serve a Greater Good or Is It an End in Itself?

Sometimes the change literature of higher education puts collaboration forward as an end in itself. We believe that in order to produce ideal conditions for collaboration, a greater good, a higher value needs to guide the choices that leaders make. The process of becoming a student-ready campus is value-laden in that way. That is why we are stressing values formation or clarification as a leadership process and recommending a democratic and horizontal approach. If a gathering consensus on campus supports the process of becoming student-ready, then collaboration should follow more smoothly than it would in the absence of that vision and set of values.

Senior leaders sometimes forget that their place in the hierarchy can silence other people. If senior leaders open meetings to more participants and don't consciously address power dynamics, they may stifle expression, creativity, and collaboration (Kezar & Lester, 2009, p. 120). Consider what would happen if you—whatever your position—open your meetings on student-readiness and empower people who might not otherwise speak to make contributions.

A positive regard for all employees as educators and leaders can become an aspect of the character or ethos and value system of the campus. Values-based leadership can become a natural practice for people who find a new place for themselves in the community or the ecosystem of the campus—and of the campus within its broader communities. Not everyone will find such a place, but as the examples that follow illustrate, some campuses are opening doors to leadership to people who might not otherwise have thought of their position in that way. While it is not our intent to recapitulate the management literature on distributed leadership models, we do recommend that senior administrators consider such advice as Robert Kegan and Lisa Laskow Lahey offer in *Immunity to Change: How to Overcome It and Unlock the Potential in Yourself and Your Organization* (2009). As Kegan and Lahey recommend, individuals in the top tier of authority, with responsibility for the entire institution, can renew their efforts to distribute responsibility and to encourage shared authority in line with the institutional mission. We would add that as a matter of principle, senior leaders may choose to exercise their power in a productive and cooperative way—creating what one might call productive tension—with the faculty and staff who are working at the grassroots level, from the bottom up.

Collaborative Leadership for Grassroots Empowerment

Research conducted at AAC&U points in this direction. The association's *Peer Review* offers an article titled "Collaborative, Faculty-Led Efforts for Sustainable Change," by senior fellow Ann S. Ferren and AAC&U staff members Rebecca Dolinsky and Heather McCambly. "Because colleges and universities are relatively flat organizations, somewhat fragmented by departmental boundaries, leadership is distributed," they observe (Dolinsky, Ferren, & McCambly, 2015, p. 30). While we would suggest that the degree of flatness may be relative, the general observation is valuable. Distributed leadership carries more potential within institutions of higher education than it does in other organizations. The idea is to make the most of distributed leadership in service of a vision of the campus as a student-ready place. In addition to reviewing the literature on effective leadership, the article recommends

- Collaborative leadership across departments and divisions
- Use of social networks to initiate and diffuse change
- Team-based learning for innovation and action

In addition to envisioning a distributed top-down, bottom-up leadership model, senior administrators can take practical steps to invite all people who work on the campus to regard themselves as educators and leaders. We recognize that this may be a new set of steps to take. But we believe it can make a significant difference to campus culture and allow for the growth of student-ready leadership in a far more democratic, developmental, and distributed way throughout the institution. Because the goal—indeed, often the highest goal—of most institutions is student learning and student success, the status of educator is clearly higher than the status of other roles. Distributing this role and responsibility can be powerful. It can offset the tendency to create a stratified caste system on campus. It can be even more powerful if the effort to share leadership connects explicitly to the diversity and equity goals of the campus.

Every Employee an Educator

All individuals who work on the campus can understand themselves to have leadership and educational roles within the enterprise as a whole. But they need to be invited to regard themselves in this way. Valencia College (2015b), for example, presents its faculty development page in a highly inclusive way—addressing all faculty as "learning leaders" no matter the type of contract they have, and beginning explicitly with adjunct and associate faculty. Among innovations available through the faculty development toolkit of resources are a peer mentoring program called "Learning Partners" and a set of professional development courses, some offering certificates, through the Teaching/Learning Academy (Valencia

College, 2014). These resources are available to any employee. The theoretical platform for this outreach incorporates Jean Lave and Etienne Wenger's influential work on communities of practice and situated learning (Lave & Wenger, 1991; Smith, 2003).

Inclusive Professional Development

A campus that intends to become ready for students may begin by reaching out to all faculty. We recommend a serious and concerted effort to improve professional development opportunities, particularly for faculty who work on term or contingent contracts. If your institution has never studied working conditions, types of teaching assignments, and access to professional development across the array of the changing faculty on your campus, now is a good time to start. To make your campus ready for students, you will need to know who is teaching the most vulnerable students on you campus how to read, write, and reason with numbers and who is helping these students to progress intentionally through their programs. You will need to make critical decisions about allocation of resources—but you will not be alone, and you will not be starting from scratch. The Delphi Project on the Changing Faculty and Student Success (2014) offers a principled and practical set of resources and campus examples that can help you get started.

This is what we mean by an intentional top-down, bottom-up strategy. It can be uncomfortable to discuss, but there is a hierarchy on campuses with a bias toward academic affairs and tenure-track faculty and a lower place for people who teach on term contracts or work for the physical plant, with student affairs typically falling somewhere in between. Yet many of the adults who hold lower-hierarchy positions possess compassion, creativity, and wisdom as educators, and they are especially talented in working with students whose origins might be similar to theirs. In particular, the people who work on the operations side of campus may be more racially and ethnically diverse than the faculty and senior administration and/or may not have attended college. Robert Sternberg's *Wisdom, Intelligence, and Creativity Synthesized* (2003) offers helpful guidance on identifying and applying the many different strengths of all members of the institutional community. If you invite staff colleagues across the institution to join in leadership and make the invitation genuinely to join the community of educators for the sake of student success, for the sake of becoming a student-ready college, you might witness an amazing outpouring of talent. In our work on campuses, we have observed this effect in the smiling faces of people welcomed for the first time to think of themselves as educational leaders.

Exemplary Practice: The University of Wisconsin-Whitewater

The University of Wisconsin-Whitewater (UW-W) exemplifies a commitment like that just described. UW-W has begun to realize the untapped potential for teaching and mentoring in the minds and hearts of staff members, especially staff members who may not have gone to college. The university has intentionally invited everyone who works on the campus to be an educator. The campus has its own LEAP

Figure 2.1   University of Wisconsin-Whitewater staff
employers help student employees understand the value of
their liberal education on the job

Source: Craig Schreiner, UWW photographer, 2015.

initiative, connected to the national work that AAC&U has
led through the LEAP initiative since 2005. Key to the work
is a student-employment program that is learning centered
and that aligns with academic programs (see Figure 2.1).
Behind this work is an explicit and mission–driven commitment to educate and empower students—a deep belief
in student capacities. Students who are employed through
work-study—for example, in the University Center, the student
center, and dining hall—are expected to learn a curriculum
developed by staff members, emphasizing practical skills such
as making change—literally, handling cash transactions—and
practicing intercultural communication (Association of
American Colleges and Universities [AAC&U], 2012). The

"LEAP HOME" pages of the university website highlight the commitment to engage all employees and welcome them to participate as educators: "Whitewater faculty and staff are passionate about sharing knowledge, fostering engagement in the community, and teaching life skills that help students prepare for the work force and become immersed in our local and global communities" (University of Wisconsin-Whitewater, 2015). For additional resources, see http://www.uww.edu/leap/faculty-and-staff-resources.

As we have suggested already, it is worth considering that the new majority of students, especially first-generation students, may have more in common with the multicultural, multigenerational people who work on buildings and grounds and in food services than with the faculty. Yet do these employees consider themselves educators? Chances are that they do not. Would they enjoy being invited to be educators? We believe so.

Exemplary Practice: California State University, Fullerton

California State University, Fullerton has taken this kind of thinking to heart. CSUF stands out for its commitment to student learning and for equitable achievement of learning outcomes across its diverse populations, as well as for community responsibility and commitment to meet these goals. The institutional mission statement begins with this sentence: "Learning is preeminent at California State University, Fullerton" (California State University, Fullerton, n.d.b). The current strategic plan, 2013–2018 lays out key objectives that begin with the academic and professional success of the diverse student body. The university presents its own diversity as a resource and openly discusses achievement gaps among student populations. Goal 2 of the strategic plan goes to the heart of the matter: "Improve student persistence, increase graduation rates University-wide, and narrow the achievement gap for underrepresented students" (California State University, Fullerton, n.d.a, p. 9). To reduce the gap, the university is intentionally using high-impact practices to promote student engagement and improve success.

With the leadership of President Mildred Garcia, CSUF has opened a series of town hall events keyed to the strategic plan. The spring 2015 Town Hall convened university faculty, staff, and students to engage in a conversation about the plan, about high-impact educational practices (HIPs) for all students, and about other university priorities. Describing the event, Vijay Pendakur, associate vice president of the Division of Student Affairs, writes, "We're serious about HIPs. At our last university-wide Town Hall Gathering, high-impact practices were a key item on the agenda. When I looked out at the audience of over 500 faculty, staff, and students, I remember seeing people from buildings and grounds crews seated in the front row of tables" (personal e-mail, June 30, 2015).

Positive Vision of Educators

This example suggests something we have seen every time we have a chance to address a mixed group of faculty, administration, and staff employees. It's refreshing and inspiring to see highly positive responses coming from staff who are typically not invited to consider themselves as educators. It helps to consider how staff members, including those who may not have attended college, may be thinking about education and social mobility, about the opportunities the institution can offer. It follows that student employment and mentoring programs are a viable and practical place to begin a broader collaboration with staff members who truly are committed to student success. Working tirelessly to strengthen relations between academic affairs and student affairs is an excellent strategy for many campuses, as has long been maintained by AAC&U and other organizations such as NASPA—Student Affairs Administrators in Higher Education. We would suggest opening even more doors to staff. We know of a number of institutions that are carrying out projects of this kind. The College Enrichment Day at Prince George's Community College, Maryland, invites all employees to attend and to discover and develop their capacities as educators (Colter, 2013). Brookdale Community College, the County College of Monmouth, New Jersey, makes a stated commitment to the principle we are exploring in this chapter. In Brookdale's vision and mission statement, one finds a set of principles. Student success comes first, followed by this pledge: "One Brookdale: Brookdale values our employees and the philosophy of One Brookdale. One Brookdale represents a collective commitment by all employees to demonstrate a consistent, appropriate and comparable level of teaching and service excellence throughout the entire College, across all locations, creating a dynamic synergy of intent and action focused on student success" (Brookdale Community College, 2013, para. 6).

Building Out the Change Effort

Although the literature on higher education reform is not abundant in advice for evidence-based approaches that lead with values and community value formation in relation to governance, help is definitely available. As we have noted, Kezar and Lester (2009) suggest that campus leaders can motivate colleagues to join a change effort if the work is centered on students and seeks to build the capacity of the institution to do a better job of helping students to learn. A willingness to innovate, a commitment to egalitarianism, a genuine interest in efficiency or in making things work better in the community will also move people to action (p. 96). Lave and Wenger's (1991) work in cognitive anthropology, mentioned earlier, opens up other avenues for collaborative thinking that can be beneficial. It is rooted in American pragmatism and the pioneering efforts of Charles Sanders Peirce and John Dewey. Dewey's work has also served for a century to guide AAC&U in practices of engaged learning and liberal education. The intellectual heritage of the ideas that can be applied to the process of becoming a student-ready college, in other words, is robust and accessible, and particularly resonant to educators.

On most campuses, an inquiry into communities of practice within the campus itself might be led by social science or philosophy departments, perhaps with the help of student researchers. These are resources that administrative leaders may have overlooked. An array of ideas for campus practice that might likewise be attractive to both departments and service units is available in David M. Callejo Perez and

Joshua Ode's edited collection titled *The Stewardship of Higher Education: Re-imagining the Role of Education and Wellness on Community Impact* (2013). The collection explores stewardship for campus and community as a convergence of work for health and education, addressing leadership, campus governance, and applied scholarship. In chapter four we will explore these dimensions of community engagement within the broader communities in which the campus is situated.

Considering Whole-Person Educators

A rich heritage of thought and leadership for the student as a whole person and the concept of formation may also be drawn from lessons learned by faith-based institutions. We would suggest, such lessons can help secular institutions that want to become ready for highly diverse students. Larry A. Braskamp, Lois Calian Trautvetter, and Kelly Ward's *Putting Students First: How Colleges Develop Students Purposefully* (2006) lays out challenges and tensions that emerge when campus leaders and faculty "create campus environments that foster holistic student development" (p. xix). The book includes valuable recommendations for community enrichment and growth, with practical guidance for open conversations on difficult topics. "Service," it observes, "without reflection can perpetuate stereotypes" (p. 188). The book frames questions to guide frank and civil disputes that can have a bearing on resolution of difficult issues concerning administrative practices and governance. "What contributions are expected of faculty?" the authors ask. "Does your institution reward faculty for fulfilling these expectations such as participation in governance and involvement in the community?" (p. 190). Shared governance involves "all members of the community in deciding on its priorities—[and] includes all members of the campus community in decision-making and in creating community" (188). Similarly, since 1999 the organization called Imagining America (n.d.) has been exploring the reward structure of institutions, particularly related to tenure and promotion based on public scholarship and community engagement in the arts and humanities.

Student-Ready Mentoring

Finally, a recent guidebook for leadership in practice is *Transformative Conversations: A Guide to Mentoring Communities Among Colleagues in Higher Education* (Felten, Bauman, Kheriaty, Taylor, & Palmer, 2013). The book offers powerful and moving prompts for discussion related to the values that individual educators hold. It provides guidance to find a wellspring of energy through conversation and mentorship. We think that conversations about a student-ready campus should be transformative and should address the formation of the whole person—the formation of the student and the formation of the educator within a community. Intentional community building needs to address matters of both heart and head in ways that are inviting and safe enough to help people to take risks. Such innovative projects as Designing the Future(s) of the University at Georgetown University (Georgetown, n.d.)

are intentionally exploring the education of the whole person and extending the inquiry into the digital realm.

The Will to Apply and Practice What Works

As these examples demonstrate, it's not that we lack ideas and recommendations. What campuses need is the will to apply and practice what works. We believe that the will to work creatively within the campus community depends on an inspiring vision that dares to address people's values and their commitments. Change for the sake of change, collaboration for the sake of collaboration—these are not inspiring and inspiriting concepts. Change for the sake of accountability is even less so. But a new vision of the campus as a place ready for the students we have and the students we will have can address deeper motivations within educators, drawing on the hopes and aspirations that made them want to work on a campus in the first place.

The idea and the ideal of the student-ready campus can serve, we would argue, specifically and powerfully to crystallize a bright vision of a more just society and motivate people to invest the effort in building capacity. This understanding of the motivation for change arising internally within the individual and supported externally within the community is what we mean by an effort to lead from the inside out and from the outside in.

Guiding Questions for All Leaders

- Does the mission statement address campus readiness for students? How? How might it be altered to make this outcome explicit rather than implicit? Could you envision an exercise with a mixed group of employees—educators, administrators, faculty both tenurable and term appointed, and staff—to experiment with changes to the mission statement, as a first step?

- Does the campus ethos include an articulated regard for the campus community as a whole, as an ecosystem, both independently and in the context of its broader communities local, state, and national? Are you confident enough in your own leadership, whatever it is that you do, that you could raise this question with others in your unit or with the person to whom you report?

- Does the president offer visible and heartfelt support for distributed leadership?

- Does the campus community embrace the idea that everyone can be a leader?

- Does the senior leadership create opportunities to discuss leadership and push the boundaries of received notions of leadership? Do employees on the operations side of campus feel welcome in discussions of leadership development for all?

- What key responsibilities, structures, and practices will need to change in order to foster, support, and reward the kind of leadership envisioned here?

- Has the campus community discussed our racialized moment in history in the United States, the implications of local and national demographic trends, the local and national disparities in wealth that have a bearing on the campus community? How might you lead your campus community to see these questions as leadership challenges and opportunities in which everyone has a stake?

Student-Ready Practice of Governance

Principle Two: Shared governance can accomplish a great deal of good.

Having made your way to this point in the chapter, you will almost certainly have devoted a thought or two to institutional shared governance. You may well be thinking how all good inspirations go to languish and die in the shadow of campus bureaucracy, in the dim light of things as they are, in the zone where administration and faculty convene to govern the institution, in whatever way they do that. Having asked mixed groups of educators and administrators on many occasions—through consulting, through campus-based projects, at workshops and institutes of various kinds—what they think of the institution-alized structures of shared governance, we recognize there is some disagreement about shared governance. While some people think shared governance works, we often hear that it does not.

The higher education change literature of the past two decades has laid out the challenges to campus practices involving faculty and administrators in excruciating detail. In "Why Does the Faculty Resist Change?" John Tagg (2012) describes a tendency for administrative leaders to lay blame for failure to change at the feet of faculty. Tagg is writing generally of change related to student learning. Interestingly, he concludes by flipping an orthodoxy in a way that connects to our argument here:

> The key to designing and executing productive institutional change is not simply to build a better academic mousetrap. Faculty will not beat a path to the doors of those with the best arguments. We need to not only design change for our institutions but redesign our institutions for change. At base, we must recognize that we can't change without changing. We cannot create a better future unless we are willing to embrace a future that is different from the past. (p. 15)

There is, Tagg recognizes, no magic bullet or simple fix, no single management strategy that will suffice to bring comprehensive institutional change. Tagg argues that the key is to address rewards, or what he calls "endowments": practices of hiring, promotion, retention, tenure; the philosophy of individualism, which undercuts collaboration; the dominance of research agendas within departments and across the institution. He concludes that we need to "create structures through which large numbers of faculty can design the change" (p. 15). By this he means to shape or create the "endowments" of the future.

Exemplary Practice: Alverno College

One exemplar Tagg chooses is Alverno College (as cited in Mentkowski, 2000). For more than a century, Alverno College has cultivated a community-wide belief in the capacities of women. Alverno has also stood the test of time as a model institution centered on learning, on demonstration of student learning outcomes and student abilities—beginning with a celebrated paradigm shift they made in the 1970s (Alverno College, 1994; 2001, p. 2). Over the past four decades, the college has earned a highly respected record of success in educating women of color in particular, with 40 percent of students so identifying. On the strength of its mission and achievement over the years, Alverno can claim to reflect the diversity of Milwaukee and its region better than any other institution (Alverno, n.d.a).

Critically important to the ethos of the college is the fact that its mission expresses a commitment to the individual learner. Alverno presents itself directly as an institution ready for students. The college tells the prospective student consistently and clearly, in public documents and on the institutional website, that she has talents and that she can learn, inviting her to imagine herself as valuable and successful and helping her to see that she will become part of a social community in which she can grow. The ethos of respect for the individual and her learning coalesces within the relationships of the community and its values. As that ethos has flourished, so the community has grown, its flourishing reflected in the diversity of the graduates.

Alverno is also an institution that has succeeded in getting faculty involved through an institutional design for change including curriculum and governance as they moved to pioneer development of a student experience directed to achievement of learning outcomes.

Outcomes for the major provide a goal for the curriculum but do not, by themselves, provide coherence. When faculty sit down as a department, we do more than establish exit outcomes for the graduate. We also work to articulate the developmental nature of the abilities. We teach toward the exit outcomes and assess students' ability to demonstrate them in developmentally appropriate ways at each stage of the curriculum, from the very first general education course to the senior seminar directly preceding graduation . . . . Ultimately, however, coherence depends as much on our practice of having every faculty member in the department teach courses at every stage as it does on the curriculum planning itself. Because each of us knows the entire curriculum, we can assist students to apply what they have learned previously.

(Alverno College, 1994; 2001, p. 3)

The change Alverno made in creating an ability-based curriculum specifically addressed faculty shared responsibilities as well as governance and rewards, including promotion and tenure (Engelmann, 2007; Mentkowski, 2000, pp. 359–405). And as this example also implies, the motivation for change was explicit and contextualized. Alverno has made an explicit commitment to be ready for the students they have and will have. Their institutional designs for learning and student success have been highly innovative, decades ahead of the curve. They have understood how to make structural changes to endowments with these goals and in this context—and how to collaborate programmatically throughout the curriculum as they share responsibility.

As the success of the learning outcomes and assessment movement in higher education has grown, practices similar to Alverno's are being developed across all types of institutions. As AAC&U's 2015 Member Survey has discovered, 85 percent of member institutions report that they have a common set of intended learning goals or learning outcomes that apply to all undergraduate students (up from 78 percent in 2008) (Hart Research Associates, 2015). The example of California State University—Monterey Bay (CSUMB), which follows, illustrates the way that the learning outcomes and assessment movement has influenced institutional practice at the program level. As in the example of Alverno College, all departments at CSUMB take responsibility for supporting the defined learning outcome for all students. This kind of design exemplifies a structural and programmatic activity supported by administration and governance that addresses a need to make the college ready for all students.

Collaboration in Practice: Institution-Wide Learning Outcomes Strategy

California State University—Monterey Bay has adopted an institution-wide graduation requirement for service learning addressing critical civic literacy. "Distinct from a traditional civics approach, critical civic literacy emphasizes the role of power in facilitating or inhibiting meaningful participation in decision making and civic life. As all departments at CSUMB have to develop service-learning courses, critical civic literacy is integrated into the core knowledge base of each of the degree programs. The departments themselves have had to wrestle with issues of diversity and social justice in new ways as they have developed their service-learning courses" (Calderón & Pollack, 2015, p. 17).

Beyond Change as a Motivator in Itself

As the examples of Alverno College and CSUMB also suggest, change as a motivator—in and of itself—is not sufficient to trigger change. The change needs to serve a meaningful vision.

Much anxiety drives higher education toward change in our era. But a generalized sense that business as usual must change is unlikely to motivate educators. Even if one puts first as a goal the achievement of student learning outcomes, the concept of change, and especially change to endowments, remains amorphous, self-directed, or circular—hardly inspirational. As the example of Alverno suggests, the motivation for change needs to speak to people, to address the actual people at the center of attention—the students—and the people who will have to take responsibility for enacting change—the faculty and staff. The motivation needs to flow from heartfelt commitment to the human, humane, faith-based, or civic responsibility of the institution.

In short, people on your campus have to care about making change. Beyond a generalized desire for reform, assuming that the intended change should improve student learning outcomes, what are the higher motives? Change in the service of what? It's worth considering what a vision of the context for change itself might be and how that vision might guide action for serious modification to endowments, shared governance, and related administrative practices where you work and lead. This approach to change and reform may be sensitive and responsive to context, may be situated, and may be visionary. It may likewise respect the ecology or ecosystem of the campus within its communities.

Here is what we recommend. The motivation for change has to be something articulated and clear, something that people can envision and embrace. The concept of "student learning" on its own is simply not powerful enough. Neither is the concept of change as a vague preparation for an uncertain future. What can be far more powerful is a new vision of students and a new vision of educators, including those faculty who work on term contracts and staff educators with the least status who are likely to be working with the most vulnerable students. Meeting people where they are right now and moving forward collaboratively with the vision of the student-ready campus is a powerful way to begin. Then, we believe, the "endowments" can begin to fall into place. Change can appear in service of a robust vision. As the urgencies and crises of our times—especially intergroup strife and the yawning socioeconomic gap—are telling us, we need brave and hopeful leaders to get started right now. There is no waiting for a perfect time. We doubt a perfect time will ever arrive, and there is far too much at stake. You might want to think in terms of educational leadership as a movement for civil rights and social mobility.

We know of no campus on which shared governance is completely dysfunctional, where no shred of potential exists to move in the direction we suggest here. If you want your institution to evolve, to be ready for the students you have and will have, you can begin to address the processes you use to govern yourselves, particularly the processes that rest in whole or in part in the hands of faculty and staff right now. The vision of a student-ready campus can guide you to address cultural change.

A Pragmatic Approach to Shared Governance

To become a student-ready campus, a campus community may find it helpful to approach shared governance in a pragmatic way and to be mindful of community members' beliefs and attitudes. Consider that people's views of shared governance are both ideologically and historically formed. Orthodoxies inflect viewpoint. You may accept widely held views that shared governance on your campus is not shared at all but a slough of despond, uselessly bogged down in politics. On the other hand, you may work at a place with robust shared governance, in which ideas and actions are subject to productive debate and action. If you begin by understanding where your campus is situated developmentally, so to speak, you can lay out and investigate a set of orthodoxies related to shared governance appropriate for your context. That approach will give you a place to begin. Changing shared governance is cultural change. You need to identify the guiding beliefs that surround the institution of shared governance on your campus and the state of well-being generally of your campus before you make a plan to alter those beliefs in a generative way to be ready for students. Context matters.

You may, for example, conclude that faculty and administration inhabit different planets and cannot communicate and that the pattern of miscommunication has become an orthodoxy in itself. It is just the way things are. But you might consider what happens when people contemplate the orthodoxy from a different angle. Imagine that the college's readiness for students, and for the thriving of a highly diverse student body, is the highest good. What happens to that good when communication among educators is thwarted at every turn? Everyone is harmed. Students are particularly vulnerable when faculty and administration don't communicate. Yet what if cooperation between faculty and administration became a new orthodoxy, something that you can say openly you want to achieve? Energy, ideas, and resources could multiply through work undertaken together. Rich and spirited communication actually could model highly functional community behavior for students.

We have recommended an intentional top-down and bottom-up, inside-out and outside-in approach to leadership that is specifically inclusive of all campus constituencies. To offer advice on your campus on the roles and responsibilities of administrators, faculty, and staff through shared governance, you will definitely need to take into account the array of endowments within your context: educators' roles and rewards, the changing nature of faculty work, and the changing characteristics of educators. You will need to be particularly aware of the dynamics of change from the inside out. Once the campus leadership has committed to becoming ready for students and recognized the potential of everyone who works on a campus to contribute as a leader, a vista of complexity will no doubt appear. That result is inevitable and necessary. But if you talk with leaders on other campuses, you will find that you are in no way alone. A positive outlook on the campus as a functioning administrative entity can be practical and helpful. Governance and policy can change, and sometimes quite dramatically.

A Vision of a Place Ready for Students

Let's assume your campus community has embraced a vision of itself as a place ready for students. Let's further assume the community accepts the idea of starting where the campus is right now and collaborating with other campuses, guided by a vision of a greater good. Every willing campus doubtless will take a different plan and pathway to make itself ready for students. Every plan worth its salt will be multifaceted. But there needs to be a coherent vision aligned with the institutional mission and a commitment to wrestle with and discuss campus values.

Having identified your orthodoxies and assessed the well-being of your campus, you should consider coming together to talk about the values you share as a community. Discussion of mission can serve this purpose. We have discovered that the LEAP Essential Learning Outcomes offered for discussion in light of the campus mission can jumpstart serious discussion. The LEAP Essential Learning Outcomes are:

Knowledge of Human Cultures and the Physical and Natural World

- Through study in the sciences and mathematics, social sciences, humanities, histories, languages, and the arts

Focused by engagement with big questions, both contemporary and enduring

Intellectual and Practical Skills, including

- Inquiry and analysis
- Critical and creative thinking
- Written and oral communication
- Quantitative literacy
- Information literacy
- Teamwork and problem solving

Practiced extensively, across the curriculum, in the context of progressively more challenging problems, projects, and standards for performance

Personal and Social Responsibility, including

o Civic knowledge and engagement—local and global
o Intercultural knowledge and competence
o Ethical reasoning and action
o Foundations and skills for lifelong learning

Anchored through active involvement with diverse communities and real-world challenges

Integrative and Applied Learning, including

o Synthesis and advanced accomplishment across general and specialized studies

Demonstrated through the application of knowledge, skills, and responsibilities to new settings and complex problems. (Association of American Colleges and Universities, n.d.a, para. 2)

The essential learning outcomes (ELOs) were themselves developed through a process like the one we are recommending here, in conversations on hundreds of campuses across the country over more than a decade (Association of American Colleges and Universities, 2007). If you have never tried to find common ground on student learning outcomes through your shared governance bodies, such as faculty or staff senates, now is a good time to start. It is likely to be helpful, critically so, to position the ELOs in service of making the campus ready for students. The University of Nebraska-Lincoln did something very similar when it used the ELOs thoughtfully and strategically to coalesce the will on campus to change general education. In the process, they made valuable discoveries about diversity and inclusion in practice and took steps that seemed revolutionary. This strategy and process might be adaptable to your own campus (Kean, Mitchell, & Wilson, 2008).

Consider the value of assembling a cross-functional and intentionally diverse leadership group that can lay out the process of discussing student learning outcomes as key to a more just and democratic pluralistic society. Think seriously about creating learning communities of educators or communities of practice that are committed to the vision of the student-ready campus as a civic responsibility (Kezar, 2015, pp. 2, 19). Learning communities and communities of practice may be powerful when guided by a vision of well-being for diverse students and educators.

Leaders who seriously want to make change should be bold enough to ask probing and meaningful questions and to launch activities that serve the broader vision to make the campus ready for students. Next, we suggest some key planning questions that these leaders may use to guide their efforts. These questions are not new; they frequently appear in the literature on change leadership on campus. See, for example, Paul L. Gaston and Jerry G. Gaff's *Revising General Education—and Avoiding the Potholes* (2009). Particularly instructive is the list of fifty potholes, into which you do not want to fall, and a list of associated pothole patches. A few examples convey the sage humor of the book: "Pothole 3: Expect a holistic change.... Patch 3: Consider the advantages of evolutionary change" (pp. 8, 31). "Pothole 46: Ignore the reward structure.... Patch 46: Endeavor to align the reward structure with the priorities of general education" (pp. 27, 33). What's different is that we invite you to ask these planning questions in service of an explicit vision of a more just society in which diverse groups of students can thrive and diverse educators can likewise flourish.

Guiding Questions for All Leaders

- Does the campus have a cross-functional and diverse team that can address campus readiness for students in the searching way that we are recommending?

- Are members of the planning team highly respected by the various sectors of the community? If they are not highly respected, the work of the team will not be held in esteem.

- Is the team relatively independent and unencumbered by the conservative tendencies of standing committees to keep the status quo? Is it charged to function as a respected ad hoc body?

- Does the team have a workable timeline, reasonable resources, and unambiguous support from the top?

- Is senior leadership committed to taking the time needed, given the overall state of the campus, to support this work?

- Is the senior leadership ready to strike a balance, sometimes standing up to speak and act and sometimes sitting on the sidelines so that others are empowered?

We don't intend to make a comprehensive list of planning questions. But we do intend to illustrate a planning process that ought to seem familiar. Importantly, such a planning process begins at the very outset to open the doors of governance with respect for the processes of the institution. Altering the culture of a campus toward student readiness requires nothing less. Sooner or later, campus governing bodies such as the senate(s) will need to be engaged; campus policies will need to change. The sooner campus leadership gets moving with governance and administrative functions, the better and wiser that leadership will be.

We would like to suggest some ways in which leadership to make the campus ready for students may open up unexpected administrative and governance functions and processes. While no one campus is likely to take up the full set of questions below, cultural change will require serious consideration of several of these questions. Over time, campus leaders may need to develop answers and plans for addressing each one.

1. Has the institution, including administrators and key governance bodies, taken a close and searching look at who is teaching undergraduate students? If leaders do not know, for example, who is teaching students to write, who is teaching general education courses, who is teaching developmental courses, it may be difficult to bring about meaningful change. If graduate students or faculty working on part-time contracts are teaching most of these courses, the institution will have trouble becoming student ready. The Delphi Project on the Changing Faculty and Student Success has developed many resources to help campuses answer critical questions about support of faculty who teach on term contracts, especially part-time assignments.

Taking the time to collect and disaggregate data on who is teaching what to whom can be a crucial strategy. Taking the time to begin working through policy and governance to change the way teaching assignments are being allocated is essential. If leaders don't take the time to figure out who is teaching the most vulnerable students, the plan for student readiness is not going to work.

2. Has leadership connected the intended change in the direction of readiness for students to the reward structures of the institution? As Kezar (2015) has observed, it is essential to "align role changes with evaluations and rewards." *Achieving Systemic Change: A Sourcebook for Advancing and Funding Undergraduate STEM Education* (Fry, 2014) builds robust support for changing faculty and institutional reward structures in order to produce an impact on student learning, especially in light of the "alarming" loss of student talent in the science, technology, engineering, and mathematics (STEM) fields (p. 3).

3. Have personnel practices for retention, reappointment, promotion, and tenure been aligned with or connected to institutional goals for student learning outcomes and to student achievement of those outcomes? Have you reviewed these documents with readiness for students in mind? Personnel policies and practices are often handled separately and apart within administration and governance. How might they be brought together with mission, vision, and programmatic practices? Can the connection be strengthened? How and where are teaching and learning considered within retention, tenure, and promotion documents? How do policies concerning the

scholarship of teaching and learning embrace the values associated with the student-ready campus?

4. How can rewards of other kinds—teaching awards and activities sponsored by centers for teaching and learning—be redesigned to address the values and goals of a student-ready campus? Excellent resources are available through the Professional and Organizational Development (POD) Network (POD, 2007–2015).

5. Is it feasible to engage faculty and staff senates or bargaining units in a discussion of rewards, including merit pay? Are rewards available to faculty on term or contingent contracts? Is discussion of rewards open to faculty and educators of all kinds, including those who work on term or contingent contracts?

6. Have you opened discussions of roles and rewards at the department level? A new publication by the New American Colleges and Universities, titled *Redefining the Paradigm: Faculty Models to Support Student Learning* contains excellent advice, readily applied within the context of a student-ready campus. The book offers chapters devoted to holistic departmental planning focused on student learning and to new approaches to faculty evaluation (Hensel, Hunnicutt, & Salomon, 2015).

7. Have you made revisions to the faculty handbook to reflect the values you place on being ready for students? The Centre College Faculty Handbook (Centre College, 2014) offers useful language, for example, on effective teaching:

"Effective teaching involves caring for students as persons; stimulating interest in the Faculty member's subject; promoting students' mastery of the facts, theories, and methods of the Faculty member's subject; encouraging students to learn independently; helping students improve skills in thinking, writing, and speaking; assisting students in identifying and clarifying the values that infuse learning; and encouraging students to become creative, responsible members of society" (Section III, pp. 1–2).

8. Can you find ways to address academic freedom in the context of a student-ready campus? Some thoughtful and readily adapted recommendations appear in *The Future of the Professoriate: Academic Freedom, Peer Review, and Shared Governance,* by Neil W. Hamilton and Jerry G. Gaff (2009). The book suggests enhancements to academic freedom that are grounded in student success. It recommends that we seek strong mechanisms for linking academic freedom to faculty responsibility. We can "root [academic freedom] in the transcendent value of educating students for a complex society as well as in the scholarly and research activities of faculty" (p. 28). We can "extend academic freedom to all who teach students to think critically about controversial and contested topics" (p. 28). Certainly the student-ready campus offers challenging prompts for seeking these connections.

9. Have you looked for opportunities voiced in the current institutional strategic plan? For example, Rochester Institute of Technology's plan offers a set of criteria for change of "silo culture" and rewards.

Difference Maker v.2
RIT will reduce academic and administrative silos and diminish the lingering negative effects of a silo culture.

Objective V.2.1
Reward collaboration within and across colleges with regard to curricula, teaching, research, and the student-faculty-staff culture. (Rochester Institute of Technology, n.d., p. 30)

Conclusion: A Vision to Guide Collaboration

Many higher education planning guides extol the value of collaboration. We do indeed endorse collaboration. But as an end in and of itself, collaboration is insufficient to motivate people to make change, especially the kind of structural change under discussion in this chapter. When the desire and impetus to collaborate emerges from shared values and a commitment to begin a process of change in service of a vision, then people will work together on the toughest challenges, especially those related to the governance of an institution. Collaboration for its own sake is unlikely to move hearts and minds. It will not inspire people to care. But collaboration *for something that people value* is attractive and generative. A strong and resonant vision provides social and emotional support to the community that shares it and gives them strength to keep on trying. On the student-ready campus, that vision can imagine an environment in which equity moves to the center of attention, and social justice and upward mobility can be ideas that people can voice. That kind of vision can move change. The more robust the values of the work, the bolder the idea, the more it will stir the passions of educators.

CHAPTER·THREE

Making Excellence Inclusive to Support Student Success

Guiding Questions

- How can educators build an intentional and supportive environment for students that reinforces that every student is known, respected, supported, and valued?

- What institutional policies and practices need to be reexamined and changed to alleviate barriers to student engagement and success?

- How are institutions preparing all students for the kind of challenges they will confront in life, work, and citizenship?

Becoming a student-ready college is a value proposition. It is an aspiration that campus leaders want to achieve, but one that does not ignore the challenges facing the enterprise of higher education, individual institutions, and educators. Becoming a student-ready college prioritizes the desire of educators to better serve our country's diverse student population. It represents a paradigm shift that reframes the conversations about student success from a mindset focused on student deficits and limitations to approaches that focus on students' assets, institutional responsibility, and personal accountability that can lead to sustainable change. However, without clearly defined action steps, "becoming a student-ready college" will quickly become one of the many catch phrases in higher education that everyone agrees with but no one really understands.

In chapter one, we provided a profile of 21st-century college students and outline some of the external market forces that may hinder the ability of higher education professionals to focus on designing a student-ready college. The educational inequities presented in chapter one are systemic and are the result of decades of policies that have disenfranchised many Americans. We do not seek in this book to address the social policies that contribute to educational disparities. Instead, we focus on strategies that can be applied when students arrive on college campuses—strategies that every educator can implement to change the institution's environment to support student success. In chapter two, we provided recommendations for how leaders can create a campus environment that encourages success for all students, starting with individual accountability and ending with collective action toward shared goals.

This chapter outlines key steps as they relate to the various roles of the participants in the ecosystem in designing campus action plans to support student learning and success. The term "ecosystem" is the best analogy to describe the symbiotic relationship among educators at individual institutions. If we think of postsecondary institutions as an ecosystem, then we are envisioning an entity that can excel through individual action and shared responsibility. Each person plays a role and must take personal responsibility for the effectiveness of that role in supporting student success. From highlighting the importance of caring educators in students' lives to defining student success and providing thought-provoking questions for institutional self-study, this chapter will provide specific guidelines for how to become a student-ready college by making excellence inclusive.

Making Excellence Inclusive

As a guiding principle of the Association of American Colleges and Universities' signature initiative, Liberal Education and America's Promise (LEAP), Making Excellence Inclusive (MEI) "is designed to help colleges and universities integrate diversity, equity, and educational quality efforts into their missions and institutional operations ... [it is] an active process through which colleges and universities achieve excellence in learning, teaching, student development, institutional functioning, and engagement in local and global communities" (AAC&U, n.d.b). Making excellence inclusive encourages institutional self-assessment and requires shared responsibility for improvement efforts and high levels of accountability—all of which describes what it means to be a student-ready college. The examples, guiding questions, and recommendations included in this chapter translate the theory of inclusive excellence into campus practice.

Removing Systemic Barriers and Challenges for Students

A young woman, age 24, who recently completed her service in the armed forces, decides to return to her local community college to complete her requirements for transfer to a four-year institution. She attended the community college prior to her enrollment in the armed forces, but completed only the first level of her developmental coursework and nine hours of credit-bearing courses. She follows the steps outlined in the student handbook for re-enrollment, but encounters roadblocks at almost every point in the re-enrollment process.

Her first stop is the admissions office. Before she can explain why she would like to speak with an admissions counselor, the receptionist stops her mid-sentence and asks for her student identification number. When she can't remember it, the receptionist asks for her social security number, without looking up to make eye contact. The receptionist tells her to take a seat and that a counselor will be with her shortly. After an hour wait and similarly disengaged conversation with an admissions counselor who confirms that her admissions paperwork is in order, the student proceeds to the advising center to register for classes. When she arrives at the advising center, she is told there is a problem with her veterans' benefits and she needs to go to the financial aid office to resolve the problem. She walks across campus to the financial aid office to meet with a counselor familiar with processing post–GI Bill benefits. Unfortunately, before she can explain her situation, the financial aid staff member asks her for her student identification number, and after accessing her records, tells her to take a seat. She waits for 30 minutes before someone tells her no one is available to help her because the one person trained to work with veterans is out of the office for the next two weeks. She is told to return at that time.

Her frustration mounts. She feels discouraged and attempts to see a faculty member from one of her developmental classes with whom she felt she connected a couple of years ago. When she reaches the office of the faculty member, she is disappointed to learn that the person is no longer in that position and has left the college for another institution. The student leaves the college without re-enrolling. When she arrives home, she decides she must say something, because this process does not encourage students to pursue their postsecondary education. She writes a letter to the president of the college and describes her day. Instead of signing the letter with her name, she signs it with her student identification number. The next day she sends the letter to the president and waits for a response.

She is surprised when she receives a call from the president within a week of sending the letter. The first thing the president does is address her by her name and ask her how she can help. The student explains her situation to the president. The president promises her that when she returns to campus the next day, her experience will be different, and there will be a person from the advising office to assist her with navigating the re-enrollment process. Before ending the call, the president asks her why she signed the letter with her student identification number and not her name? She shyly responds, "Because that is the first thing everyone asked me when I wanted help, and I knew you would be able to find me faster with my student identification number. It is my identity at the college. My name doesn't matter."

This hypothetical story draws on details from true experiences. It is not meant to place blame on any particular office on a college campus. It describes a set of circumstances and responses that can occur in any office on a college campus. Unfortunately, it also reflects the informal and formal conversations we have had with too many underserved students in higher education during campus visits. The questions readers should ask in response to this story are "Does this happen on my campus? Could this happen at my campus? Have I ever treated a student in a similar manner?"

A Caring Educator

As an unintended consequence of external incentive structures that prioritize institutional efficiency in higher education (i.e., completion-driven financial reward systems), our core beliefs and values about what we, as educators, know are the critical elements for student success are being overshadowed. Becoming a student-ready college requires a deep commitment to continual institutional and self-assessment. AAC&U's publication *Committing to Equity and Inclusive Excellence: A Campus Guide for Self-Study and Planning* (2015) includes ten action steps that "provide a framework for needed dialogue, self-assessment, and action" (p. 4). The first step is "knowing who your students are and will be." The second step is "committing to frank, hard dialogues about the climate for underserved students on your campus, with the goal of effecting a paradigm shift in language and actions." These two action steps are essential first steps in becoming a student-ready college because they speak to the core beliefs and values of individuals and institutions.

One of those critical elements of the campus climate is a caring educator—an element of student success that cannot be quantified or measured by an efficiency scale. Research studies have shown the power of a caring adult in the overall success of students at various ages (Harvey, 2007; Kramer & Gardner, 2007; Lerner & Brand, 2006; McClure, Yonezawa, &

Jones, 2010). In a recent Gallup survey that asked "Was there someone who encouraged your development?," responses confirmed that this assurance of encouragement remains one of the two essential factors in a person's feeling of success in work and life many years after completion of postsecondary education (Busteed, 2015).

Considering the value of a caring educator in the process of supporting student success, what is the role of the caring adult in a student-ready college? First, let us dispel the idea that we want every educator to become a "counselor" for every student he or she encounters. That is not our message, and that is an impossible aspiration, given the limits on time and effort for most educators. Our message is that within our personal sphere of influence on the college campus (e.g., students in your classroom, advisees, students who work in your office, students who access academic support services), how are our daily actions demonstrating compassion and empathy for the students we encounter? Are we understanding of the challenges and obstacles that students face today, and do we see these challenges not as reflecting students' deficits, but as reflecting the deficits of our institutions, our society, or even ourselves?

At a student-ready college, educators should strive to be empathetic. According to Bennett, "empathy is the imaginary participation in another person's experience, including emotional and intellectual dimensions, by imagining his or her perspective (not by assuming the person's position)" (as cited in Association of American Colleges and Universities, n.d.c). An empathetic educator can feel the lack of identity and isolation the student in the scenario experienced through imaginary participation in the emotional and intellectual responses that the female veteran student in this chapter's opening anecdote encountered in navigating the institutional processes for re-enrollment. This ability to personally understand and relate emotionally with the student is what motivates empathetic educators to act and to offer assistance. An empathetic educator would view the student's situation as a failing of the institution, not of the student, and would take the necessary steps to change institutional procedures to ensure that other students do not have similar experiences. Imagine if every time we encountered a student in need of assistance, we asked ourselves, "If this were my son, daughter, friend, or mentee, how would I want someone to help him or her?" Approaching each situation in this way transforms our responses to be more empathetic. Becoming a student-ready college requires each and every person who is part of the ecosystem to make a personal decision to take responsibility and ownership for student success. It requires each person to make every action, every task, every lecture, every assignment, every experience expressions of care and emotion. It means realizing that being an educator is not just a profession, a career, or a job. It means defining your role in an ecosystem as a responsibility for fostering continual improvement and for serving in a role of support and guidance for students.

Embracing a Paradigm Shift

A student-ready college does not focus solely on beliefs, values, and intent without action, specifically individual and collective action. Continual reflection is inherent and serves as a core structural process for student-ready colleges. Becoming a student-ready college requires every person to have a sense of ownership and a level of participation in the ecosystem of the institution to make it successful. Full participation requires self-examination. We must know who our students are and will be beyond the demographic data, but we must first also know ourselves as educators. The students we are educating today are more diverse than ever before. They come from various ethnic, racial, and sexual identity groups; a multitude of geographic regions; a range of age groups; and a myriad of socioeconomic backgrounds. Given the diversity of student backgrounds and the reality that it is human nature to have preconceived notions about others who are not similar to ourselves, it is critical that we, as educators, spend time recognizing and acknowledging our biases and the stereotypes that may negatively influence the students we serve.

If this self-examination does not occur, there will be a tendency to address student success and institutional change from a deficit-minded perspective, or from a perspective researchers have named "implicit bias." Estela Mara Bensimon, codirector of the Center for Urban Education and professor at the Rossier School of Education at the University of Southern California, describes deficit-minded thinking as "funds of knowledge that prevent[s] individuals from seeing racial inequity or cause[s] them to interpret disparities as a deterministic deficiency that afflicts Latinos, Latinas, and African Americans in particular" (Bensimon & Malcom, 2012, p. 30). Deficit-minded thinking involves blaming the students for being underprepared, rather than blaming the social systems that perpetuate inequities in education. It involves the belief that certain students cannot learn how to navigate the complexities of higher education, that they are unmotivated, or that they lack the intellectual capacity to succeed in certain programs. Deficit-minded thinking can extend to all student groups that are seen as different by an individual educator. The term "implicit biases" "refers to the attitudes or stereotypes that affect our understanding, actions, and decisions in an unconscious manner. These biases, which encompass both favorable and unfavorable assessments, are activated involuntarily and without an individual's awareness or intentional control. Residing deep in the subconscious, these biases are different from known biases that individuals may choose to conceal for the purposes of social and/or political correctness" (Kirwan Institute for the Study of Race and Ethnicity, 2015). For example, an educator might view students of color as lazy or as unmotivated and not as intelligent as other students, based on societal stereotypes and images perpetrated in the media. Low-income students may be seen as not having financial literacy or understanding the value of saving money—and these supposed characteristics, or deficits, might be seen as a rationale for why these students are poor. These deficit-minded thoughts, biases, and stereotypes can influence how we educate and interact with students. Becoming a student-ready college requires individuals who make up the institution's ecosystem to identify, to acknowledge, and to confront these beliefs to begin a change process that doesn't limit student opportunities for learning and success. Every educator should ask the questions, "What do I believe about students who are different from me? What are my personal beliefs about today's college students that may hinder my ability to create a student-ready college?"

Once educators have identified their beliefs, they should examine those beliefs for biases, misconceptions, and pre-conceived notions that can hinder student learning and success. This level of acknowledgment and self-examination seems counterintuitive to how educators perceive themselves because it is generally assumed that higher education pro-fessionals, because of academic training and the pursuit of knowledge, are at the forefront of reflection, inclusivity, and acceptance. Unfortunately, this is not always the case. In fact, deficit-minded practices and beliefs about student success are pervasive and entrenched in campus policies and practices. We will not progress to the level of caring described earlier until we can engage in the types of conversations that can help us deal with the mindsets that limit our capacities to truly care. We all have limitations in our ability to be effective educators. It is only through open discussions and ownership of these biases, preconceived notions, and assumptions about diverse students that we can initiate the process of becoming student-ready.

One way that campuses can encourage this level of self-examination and accountability is through holding ongo-ing intergroup dialogues for all educators to explore entrenched biases and stereotypes. We are not speaking of the one-day diversity workshops that are common to most campuses; these are ongoing, intergroup dialogues or "courageous conversa-tions" for faculty, staff, and administrators that should represent a process for continual learning that will shape current and future campus conversations and lay the foundation for an inclusive and honest campus culture. Furthermore, these dialogues should not be considered opportunities to label colleagues who are honest in sharing their views; rather, the dialogues should be considered safe places for engaging in difficult conversations that will ultimately benefit the campus community. In these dialogues, colleagues can develop relationships with "critical friends" to help maintain a mutual commitment and a level of shared accountability for addressing assumptions, biases, and preconceived notions when they arise.

Guiding Questions

- How does your institution value and affirm the cultural capital of underserved students?

- What biases or stereotypes may be standing in the way?

- What do your students' own stories tell you about the work you need to do?

- How do you ensure that underserved students receive the appropriate amount of challenge and support to ensure their success, without marginalizing these students?

- What can you learn from your own successes and failures and from other institutions working to increase underserved student success?

A Culture of Inclusion

Institution A, a regional, comprehensive four-year college, has a new president who is in the process of developing a five-year strategic plan, as the current plan ends in one and half years. The student demographics of this suburban institution have changed dramatically over the past six years: (1) the students are more ethnically and racially diverse, (2) the number of students on financial aid has risen from 25 percent to 44 percent, (3) the faculty regularly complain that the current students are not as academically prepared for college-level work as students in the past, and (4) state funding for the institution has been reduced by 2 to 3 percent every fiscal year for the past three years. One of the new president's initiatives is to create a Center for Student Success with a focus on implementing high-impact practices to increase student engagement and to advance student learning and success. The president has identified a team of campus leaders, based on areas of responsibility, to serve as the student success committee and to provide goals, objectives, and programs for the Center for Student Success. A new director for the Center has been hired and serves as the cochair of the committee, along with the vice-provost of undergraduate education and the assistant vice president of student affairs. The president has given the committee one academic year to submit a comprehensive plan for the service design of the Center.

Does this scenario sound familiar? Many campuses have instituted student success committees and elevated the role of that committee in shaping the agenda for campus change. The charge from the president is valid and is a common response on how to initiate a change process—form a committee to explore ideas and to propose a plan. However, if we seek to create student-ready colleges and we perceive the campus community as an ecosystem with individual and shared responsibilities focused on promoting collective action, then the traditional version of functioning by committee no longer fits with these efforts. The structure and use of the committee for institutional decision making can be a hindrance to a student-ready college—and antithetical to the creation of a culture of inclusion and the promotion of transparency. Functioning by use of the committee structure creates a campus culture divided between those who hold knowledge and those who do not. Consider the following questions: Who is generally chosen to serve on committees? Is it those in the inner circle of the leadership? Is it those who hold prominent titles and positions in the campus community? At a student-ready college, the traditional view of the committee is dismantled and a new role emerges. The redesigned role of the committee offers full participation, open communication, and transparency.

Instead of functioning mainly by committees, we propose a more inclusive way of sense making to generate ideas—topical dialogues and campus forums open to all faculty, staff, and administrators to explore individual perspectives and to build shared commitments and common understanding of the goals and values of the institution as well as promising practices for advancing student success. The point at which the "committee" starts in the planning process will shape every action that takes place in the design and implementation of the final recommendations. The committee's purpose is to facilitate widespread understanding of the goals and to gather input on the process, to promote collaboration among campus educators, and to develop a process that encourages and measures coordination of efforts to achieve a common goal.

Defining Student Success as Learning

In our roles at national organizations focused on improving higher education institutions and student outcomes, we have the opportunity to work with campus educators across the country who often find themselves in situations similar to the scenario just described. When speaking with a group of stakeholders, one of the first things we do is ask them to define what student success means to them and for their institution. This question is not new. Defining student success and clarifying goals are essential elements of any student success plan. That is why it surprises us that, when we ask, we still get as many different answers as there are educators in the room. A student-ready institution has a clear vision of what student success is, and that vision is known and valued across campus. It is part of the institutional culture. If it is not commonly known and valued by campus educators, then this is a critical initial charge to those leading topical dialogues and campus forums.

From our perspective, if the goal is to prepare students for the kinds of challenges they will confront in work, in life, and as citizens, both U.S. and global, and to help them integrate and apply their knowledge and skills to complex and unscripted problems, then the definition of student success at an institution is more than the institution's mission statement, graduation rates, or retention rates. It is the institutional learning outcomes. It is the learning that every student will achieve before graduating from the institution. However, even though most institutions have learning outcomes, very few are disaggregating data by student characteristics to assess whether excellence is truly inclusive (Hart Research Associates, 2015).

Educators at a student-ready college are keenly aware of the learning outcomes at their institution and the experiences through which students demonstrate achievement of these learning outcomes. They have a comprehensive assessment plan for evaluating student work products to ensure that all students are achieving the benchmarks of proficiency (e.g., AAC&U's Valid Assessment of Learning in Undergraduate Education). Students are aware of the learning outcomes that they must achieve, the relevance of these outcomes to their success, and the academic and cocurricular pathways through which they will achieve proficiency of the learning outcomes. In other words, the guided learning pathway for student success is transparent and clearly defined. A student-ready college has a plan in place to achieve these goals, and every educator on campus understands his or her role in helping to achieve these outcomes.

Guiding Questions

- What are the learning outcomes for your institution? For your department? For your program?

- How widely known are the learning outcomes among your colleagues? How are you communicating the learning outcomes to campus educators?

- Are the learning outcomes used as the definition of student success on your campus?

- How does your institution assess student achievement of the learning outcomes? Are specific student groups not achieving the learning outcomes compared to other student groups?

- Is there an assessment plan in place to track student progress with achievement of the outcomes?

- Are students aware of the learning outcomes and the relevance to their success?

- Do students know their current proficiency levels of learning outcomes? Do they have defined proficiency level goals?

- Do students know the pathways for achievement of the learning outcomes?

Promoting Excellence in Student Engagement

The president in the earlier scenario is responding to the extensive research on high-impact educational practices (HIPs), which shows that student participation, especially underserved student participation, in these educational practices (e.g., first-year experiences, common intellectual experiences, learning communities writing-intensive courses, collaborative assignments and projects, undergraduate research, diversity/ global learning, service learning, community-based learning, internships, capstone courses and projects), can lead to higher levels of student persistence and grade point averages (Kuh, 2008) and self-reported learning gains (Kuh, 2008; Kuh & O'Donnell, 2013; Finley & McNair, 2013).

In our work with campuses, we have discovered that a directive to simply implement HIPs, absent an examination of students' needs, institutional capacity, and faculty and staff development, often leads to a convoluted curriculum design and a variety of HIPs with little integration and limited effectiveness. When campus educators discuss embedding HIPs into the curriculum and cocurriculum experience, they often fail to explore intentionality in connecting the implementation of HIPs to defined learning outcomes. And as they discuss selecting, designing, and implementing HIPs, they also often overlook assessing those HIP-influenced outcomes and analyzing equity in student participation. Figure 3.1 illustrates a model for discussing the intentionality of HIPs.

The quality dimensions of high-impact practices also play a critical role in the success of these practices in increasing student achievement of learning outcomes. If implementation and scaffolding of high-impact practices across a student's educational experience form a sustainable change strategy through guided learning pathways, educators must design HIPs based on these criteria:

- Performance expectations set at appropriately high levels
- Significant investment of time and effort by students over an extended period of time

- Interactions with faculty and peers about substantive matters
- Experiences with diversity, wherein students are exposed to and must contend with people and circumstances that differ from those with which students are familiar
- Frequent, timely, and constructive feedback
- Periodic, structured opportunities to reflect and integrate learning
- Opportunities to discover relevance of learning through real-world applications
- Public demonstration of competence (Kuh & O'Donnell, 2013, p. 8)

Figure 3.1   Model for Discussing the Intentionality of HIPs

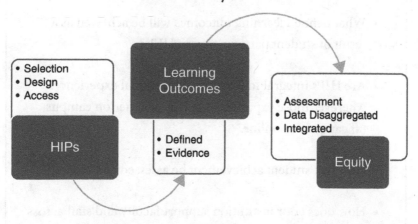

Key questions that every "committee" or campus forum should address:

- What do you want to accomplish by focusing on the design and development of HIPs?

- What are your goals for student learning and success?

- Are they tied to the institution's mission and vision for student success and retention?

- What HIPs currently exist on your campus?

- What do you know about who participates? Who has access? Who doesn't?

- What makes these practices high-impact? [*Hint: Evidence of achievement of student learning outcomes*]

- What defined learning outcomes will be achieved as a result of student participation in HIPs?

- Are HIPs integral to students' educational experiences wherever those experiences occur, whether on campus, off campus, or online?

- How will student achievement be assessed and tracked?

- How does your institution support faculty and staff across programs as they incorporate high-impact practices into their work?

Colleges that are student-ready have engaged in campus dialogues to define answers and strategies for addressing these questions. Not only are the answers clearly articulated and widely shared among campus educators, but they are also valued, and each educator understands his or her role in helping to achieve the goals—this individual responsibility leads to collective action. At a student-ready college there are numerous opportunities for reflection and examination of the goals along with the evidence of success. The intentionality of the design of the student success plan becomes transparent through an institutional culture of full inclusion and diverse perspectives.

Charting Your Course of Action

As previously stated, Making Excellence Inclusive is "an active process through which colleges and universities achieve excellence in learning, teaching, student development, institutional functioning, and engagement in local and global communities." Our experiences with campuses have helped us identify key elements of any student success plan that will help educators clearly define the various roles and responsibilities for all stakeholders:

- Clear identification and definition of the problem based on data (quantitative and qualitative)
- Content goals (the "what" you seek to achieve)
- Process goals (the "how" and the "who" will be responsible)
- Defined actions and timeline (action, purpose/details, and when)

- Measures of success, including direct assessment of student learning
- Communication with stakeholders and strategies for continuous feedback and improvement

Campuses seeking to become student-ready will address these key elements as part of their student success efforts and will engage the entire campus community in the conversations. Making Excellence Inclusive involves high levels of accountability through the use of clearly defined goals and measures of student progress and success.

Conclusion

Defining what it means to be a student-ready college starts with an individual educator and moves on to the collective action of all educators to influence and change the institutional environment to make excellence inclusive by supporting the success of all students. As important as it is to know who your students are, it is just as important for you to understand who you are as an educator and what limitations may hinder your ability to fully educate all students, especially those who are different from you. We have an individual and shared responsibility to engage in self-reflection and to hold each other accountable for our actions. We must learn to be empathetic educators and to focus on students' assets, not their deficits. Educators at a student-ready college define success by the learning outcomes students must achieve, and they provide high-quality educational experiences to help students achieve at levels that prepare them for lifelong success. A student-ready college prioritizes learning over efficiency, even when external pressures call for a different course of action. The success of students comes first.

CHAPTER·FOUR

Building Student Readiness through Effective Partnerships

Guiding Questions

- What are the essential understandings and preconditions that enable campus leaders to support their students' success by leveraging the ecosystem that surrounds their campuses?

- Who are today's college students, and what institutional and interpersonal dynamics can influence their success on college campuses?

- How can campus leaders create partnerships that work?

In this chapter we contend that student-ready colleges and universities demonstrate the willingness to use strategic partnerships with other higher education institutions, community and government organizations, and others to strengthen their on-campus capacity to support student success. This approach, which distinguishes student-ready colleges from the more traditionally "self-contained" approach of their peers, reflects a necessary vision to rewrite the dynamics of the traditional campus-student and campus-community relationships. We contend that external partnerships are an effective way to help student-ready colleges provide holistic student supports, and these supports are necessary because many of the key challenges faced by today's diverse student population (such as unmet financial need, family responsibilities, military status, age, etc.) originate outside of the classroom. We recommend that student-ready institutions first seek to identify their students' holistic needs, compare those needs to the type and number of available on-campus resources, and bolster (where needed) their institutional capacity to serve those needs by pursuing partnerships with community-based organizations, workforce boards, government agencies, faith-based organizations, and others. We contend that student-ready colleges embrace the discipline of developing, providing, and embedding holistic services to the point that this service orientation becomes part of the campus's very identity.

We open this chapter by describing a key motivation for effective campus partnerships—the understanding that the college campus is part of a larger community *ecosystem* that has both a need for the college and the resources with which to strengthen it. We follow by introducing the concept of opportunistic self-awareness, which we define as an institutional predisposition to learn about insufficiencies in on-campus service capacity and bolster that capacity by connecting with resources outside of campus. We then describe the profile of 21st-century college students and some of the ways that student-ready colleges are using external partnerships to help offset the significant—and in some ways, unprecedented— challenges to their postsecondary attainment. We conclude the chapter by offering practical suggestions for institutions that seek to increase their student-readiness by beginning and maintaining effective partnerships.

Engaging the Ecosystem

In biology, *symbiosis* refers to the interaction between two organisms of different species that live in close association with one another. While there are technically several types of symbiosis (determined by the benefits—if any—that each organism gains), the most common use of the term refers to relationships in which the survival needs of both parties benefit equally. We apply this concept to American higher education, and we state, for the sake of argument, that the structure, purpose, and function of colleges and universities qualify them as a unique "species" separate from the various for-profit, not-for-profit, governmental, and other entities in our communities. Further extending this analogy, we also argue that colleges and universities exist as part of a larger *community ecosystem*—an environment within which all of the neighboring "species" (for-profits, non-profit, governmental, etc.) function while interacting with each other and the environment. Our allegorical ecosystem also has a *climate*— the geographic, regulatory, social, financial, and other conditions that affect the entire system. Just as in nature, the specifics of this climate—inside and outside of an individual institution—profoundly impact the terms and conditions of the experience (and indeed, the very survival) of those affected by it.

Figure 4.1 illustrates a typical college or university campus and a very small cross-section of the myriad "species" and entities that occupy the space around it. It should come as no surprise that our graphic places students—residents in our communities whose postsecondary attainment helps to fuel the American economy, democracy, and social order—at the center of the system. The institution—represented by the various high-level decision makers whose choices dictate the student experience on campus—surrounds the students and serves as the membrane that receives (or blocks) the influences of the various other entities in the system.

Figure 4.1   Higher Education Ecosystem

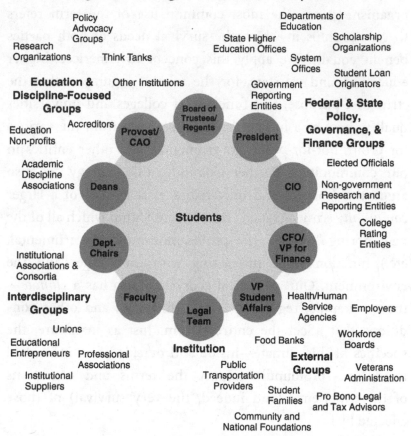

Source: Adapted from Lumina Foundation, Higher Education Landscape, 2014.

Like their biological peers, individual campuses tend to engage this populous environment according to a hardwired set of ground rules. At most institutions, these "survival instincts" favor individualism over community cooperation and engagement. These instincts were developed and maintained by decades of policies and practices that can support institutional operations when used strategically, but also, if overused, promulgate a mistaken belief that a campus is self-sufficient. This is not a condemnation of campus leadership; we recognize that the intense competition for limited financial resources and the impact of large-scale policy changes—such as outcomes-based funding, the Affordable Care Act, and the Workforce Investment and Opportunity Act (to name a few)—certainly justify a reasonable amount of institutional self-focus. We simply contend that the leaders of student-ready colleges understand that their survival is best sustained by supporting the needs of today's students in ways that run counter to the instincts of decades past—by seeking out and maximizing collaborations with other institutions and the external groups shown in the bottom right corner of Figure 4.1. These partners include workforce boards, health and human service agencies, community organizations, and others whose unique resources can help to meet some of the most pressing survival needs of today's students. In the true spirit of symbiosis, these partnerships also provide these external community partners with the benefits of access to the considerable resources that only that partnering institution can provide.

But what triggers this institutional predisposition toward student-focused symbiosis? What motivates the leaders of student-ready colleges to overcome the assumption that external partnerships are somehow impossible, impractical, or incompatible with institutional mission? The answer is an evolved survival instinct—one that recognizes institutional strength as a natural outcome of student completion (which is itself a by-product of effective student support). This perspective drives student-ready college decision makers to review qualitative and quantitative information about students to determine opportunities to improve supports for student success; to locate and connect with external partners who can help the campus to capitalize on those opportunities; and to monitor and support these partnerships in ways that ensure reciprocal benefit to partners and improvement in the services that students receive on campus.

A New Survival Instinct: The Opportunistic Self-Awareness of Student-Ready Colleges

At its core, the "opportunistic self-awareness" of student-ready colleges is a heightened sense of self-awareness derived from a steadfast commitment to student success as the inspiration and justification for proactively seeking out opportunities to expand their capacity to support students more effectively. On balance, the institutional behaviors at these institutions reflect campus-wide ownership and leadership of their responsibilities to intentionally design, deliver, and maintain the resources and culture necessary to ensure student success. Student-ready colleges operate according to a principle of social responsibility, their fidelity to which distinguishes them from other institutions. They serve all of their students across a variety of student demographics and needs. Institutions with opportunistic self-awareness are ever mindful of their own strengths and limitations—including which students benefit from or are hindered by the institutional context—and their ownership of student outcomes catalyzes their efforts to pursue, evaluate, and improve opportunities to support equitable outcomes for student success.

Research is widely available across the field of higher education about the forces within college and university environments that act on students and have implications for their success. The higher education literature is replete with research on the formal organizational dimensions of college and the informal social dimensions of college on students' experiences as well as the impact of these dimensions on students' success. Moreover, it is generally understood that a complex interplay between students' backgrounds and the organizational culture of a college or university may tend to push or pull students toward or away from an ideal state of success within an institution's academic and social communities (Tinto, 1988; Benjamin, Chambers, & Reiterman, 1993). Students begin college with a set of important orienting background characteristics—which we may or may not think of as helping or hindering student success—including characteristics such as family education level, family income, and prior academic experience and preparation (Tinto, 1975; 1988; Pascarella, 1985; Weidman, 1987). Research on the influence of institutional characteristics in the impact of a college on students has traditionally focused on institutional size, resources, and control; however, additional organizational attributes, such as mission, faculty expectations, administrative decision making/leadership, and the extracurricular environment are also important forces within colleges and universities (Weidman, 1989). More specifically, students' experiences are affected in a variety of ways by the organization and administration of college environments, including the way faculty and administrators interact with students, patterns

of administrative decision making, and organizational functioning (Berger, 2000; Bean, 1983; Berger & Braxton, 1998).
Organizational attributes such as institutional communication,
fairness in the administration of rules and policies, and the
participation of students in decision making also influence the
success or early departure of students (Braxton, 2000).

The existing analyses provide an important and useful
framework for understanding how college affects students at
a macro level, and establish the foundation for much deeper
investigation. However, they do little to clarify or systemically
explain the reasons why particular effects occur, or why the
experiences and outcomes of so many students remain uneven.
More importantly, they do little to clarify how colleges can
achieve a perpetual state of readiness and effectiveness in serving today's students. Historically, there is broad disagreement
about the implications of the larger external environment on
student success. For example, Tinto (1986) suggests that "while
external forces may influence decisions to go to college and
may greatly constrain the choice of which college to attend,
their impact on departure following entry is generally quite
minor" (p. 376). In contrast, Weidman (1984) emphasized the
importance of external influences; specifically, that institutions
of higher education are not completely encapsulated environments. Further, Bronfenbrenner (2005) argues that student
development is influenced to varying degrees by different
types of environmental systems, including systems in which
students do not directly participate but which nonetheless
exert influence over their educational contexts. And so, in
considering how colleges can be transformational in their
capacity to maximize student success, it is imperative that

colleges and universities reach forward—beyond the conventional parameters of what is already known and the grasp of questions that have already been answered, beyond the familiar conventions and traditions associated with serving yesterday's students—to fully embrace the new realities of the higher education ecosystem.

Today, efforts to increase college attainment and close equity gaps are national priorities, affecting educators' work at the state, system, and institutional levels; and the field of higher education is replete with exemplary efforts to increase student success. The current economic environment has affected the financial situation of most higher education institutions as well as operational constraints on institutional resources as a whole. The economic environment—combined with shifts in local, state, and even national demographics—has led to a higher education context in which vast numbers of institutions operate in competition with each other. Yet higher education institutions are essential to increasing educational attainment in the United States overall, and in cities across the nation. It is imperative that higher education institutions deliver on both short- and long-term goals for student success.

In order to realize the promise of higher education for today's students—to close achievement gaps and increase attainment—significant and fundamental changes must occur in the role of higher education institutions and in how we conceptualize models of organizational functioning within the 21st-century context. Specifically, while prevailing research on student success and models of practice center on single efforts within single institutional contexts, the visions of the singular, independent, insular institutions will no longer work. By embracing today's students, fueling this country's workforce, and responding to the needs of communities and of society as a whole—effectively—what student-ready colleges have mastered is the result of opportunistic self-awareness.

Student-ready colleges cultivate more effective opportunities to support the academic, social, and financial needs of their students by engaging as active participants in an ecosystem of complex, evolving organizations; by operating according to a strategic paradigm that involves understanding, respecting, and leveraging the resources of organizations across the ecosystem; and by working together to create new innovations and to shape the future.

Student-ready colleges cultivate more effective opportunities to support the academic, social, and financial needs of their students by

- Engaging as active participants in an ecosystem of complex, evolving interdependent organizations
- Operating according to a strategic paradigm that involves understanding, respecting, and leveraging the resources of organizations across the ecosystem
- Working together to create new innovations and to shape the future

Student-ready colleges understand that the central strength of their ability to serve the array of students within their institutions is manifest in *how* they leverage resources to support their students' success. Specifically, student-ready colleges are opportunistic in their capacity to act quickly and to effectively channel resources to manage their responsibilities as well as to address deficits within their context. In short, student-ready colleges know that the primary constraints on their ability to serve students are not so much the extent of their institution's resources, but rather the limits of their facility for channelling institutional and ecosystem resources consistent with their fundamental responsibilities to deliver comprehensive and productive academic, social, and financial support for students, and for leveraging resources in a manner that extends both human and financial capital. Student-ready colleges scan the landscape and forecast the changing conditions and sociocultural influences and opportunities across the ecosystem; they cultivate value-sustaining relationships and networks across the ecosystem that overlap significantly across environments and can be influenced by the interplay between contexts. It is important to note that student-ready colleges thrive in complex, dynamic, interactive ecosystems. While many institutions fall short in imagining the value-sustaining partnerships and networks across the ecosystem because they focus primarily on students who are the direct receivers of educational services, student-ready colleges consider the wide variety of publics they serve and with which they communicate and interact. Student-ready colleges tailor external communication and interaction in a way that provokes a response and cultivates a connection based on common interests and commitments. Moreover, external communication and interaction occur in a manner that is so elevated and systematic and so consistently yields results that it is practically scientific. Fundamentally, opportunistic external communication and interaction at student-ready colleges is timely, precise, appropriately nuanced, transparent, and strategic; it is ongoing; and it reflects a commitment to understanding. While it does not necessarily require agreement, it establishes understanding and common values, and it identifies the basis of a mutually beneficial exchange between student-ready colleges and their partners in the ecosystem. Thus student-ready colleges are poised to leverage the complexity and variety of the ecosystem to build external partnerships and networks that help to create, support, sustain, and enhance the learning experience and outcomes of today's students in direct response to their needs.

The Many Faces of Partnership

A variety of partnership opportunities for student-focused institutions has emerged over time. Some involve collaborations in which entire cities or regions participate in building K–16 or "cradle to career" pipelines; others feature cohorts of postsecondary institutions working as peers to solve individual and collective challenges; still others consist of a single campus improving its services to students by partnering with entities from government, not-for-profit, faith-based, or other sectors. Collaborative partnerships and alliances are two of the types of partnerships that colleges seeking to better support student success can have with members of their surrounding ecosystem. There are several organizing elements associated with collaborative partnerships, processes, and structures. In particular, Wood and Gray (1991) describe the characteristics of collaborative partnerships as interactive; intentional; involving sharing of processes, structures, and/or resources; and future-centric—especially aimed at reducing complexity and enhancing control. Moreover, the power of collaborative partnerships is established when two or more individuals, groups, or organizations join together to share information and resources to achieve an outcome that could not be accomplished by working independently (O'Brien, Littlefield, & Goddard-Truitt, 2013). Effectively, partnerships represent the commitment of different organizations to work together around common interests and to respond to a specific problem or opportunity. There can be considerable variation in how collaborative groups work, in what they do, and in the contextual constraints they encounter (Lumina Foundation, 2015b). Partnerships take many forms—commonly coalitions, networks, alliances, learning communities, and so on—and make use of or organize around collaborative infrastructures such as collective impact. The analysis of a variety of partnerships from nearly a decade of grant projects centered on collaboration at Lumina Foundation suggests a basic foundation for cultivating partnerships, including: ensuring that the right organizations are at the table; developing a set of desired outcomes; formalizing partnership expectations and contributions, including identifying a lead or "backbone" organization; and leveraging opportunities for open communication and shared learning (Lumina Foundation, 2015a). Further, student-ready colleges build partnerships that leverage the conditions within the larger system that are necessary for delivering on the mission of the institution to support and advance the success of its students.

While some partnerships form as a result of external, project-based funding from agencies or foundations, many student-ready partnerships begin as a result of the partners' recognition of the economies of scale they can achieve through collaboration. In this chapter we offer several examples of self-organized collaborative partnerships across the higher education ecosystem to improve the success of students at scale. One approach to collaboration is networked improvement communities. Bryk, Gomez, and Grunow (2010) suggest that the value of networked improvement communities can be found in their effectiveness at guiding the multiple, varied efforts needed to support collective action and to achieve improved outcomes for complex problems at scale. In particular, networked improvement communities are structured networks of organizations that intentionally come together to define and support collective action and that achieve improved outcomes for complex problem(s) at scale by working together. The networked improvement community approach described by Bryk, Gomez, and Grunow (2010) functions to the benefit of participating organizations in many ways and on multiple levels. For example, networked improvement collaboratives function as learning, design, and resource communities through which structured opportunities to identify, develop and organize, and exchange information and resources are offered; plans are executed; and agreed-upon measures of success and outcomes are monitored and shared across all of the institutions and organizations that the partnership comprises. Additionally, these collaborative partnerships can engage and benefit each partner institution and organization singly and on multiple levels, in terms of direct frontline service and teaching and instruction, and at various levels of leadership and management. While the concept of networked improvement communities in education has been borrowed from other industries, the basic framework of this form of collaboration is useful in educational contexts. Networked improvement communities in education are organized around three central ideas, which provide a basic orienting infrastructure for improvement at scale: "What are we trying to solve? Whose expertise is needed? How do we organize to achieve the outcome?" (p. 4). To advance these central ideas, networked improvement communities formalize several structural operating components, including (1) defining rules and norms of membership and participation; (2) identifying areas of common work, including priorities and timelines; and (3) developing and/or endorsing shared measurements and outcomes.

One of the most recent and compelling examples of the opportunistic self-awareness of student-ready colleges can be found in the formation of the University Innovation Alliance (UIA)—which is organized in a manner that is consistent with the structure of networked improvement collaboratives. On December 4, 2014, members of the UIA joined President Barack Obama and other higher education leaders at the White House, and pledged to graduate an additional 68,000 students by 2025. Officially, the UIA launched in September 2014, and comprises eleven public research universities—including two flagships, five land-grants, and four massive universities. Specifically, these institutions include Arizona State University, Georgia State University, Iowa State University, Michigan State University, Ohio State University, Oregon State University, Purdue University, University of California Riverside, University of Central Florida, University of Kansas, and University of Texas, Austin. These eleven public universities enroll almost 400,000 undergraduate students collectively—ranging in six-year graduation rates from 51 to 82 percent. Specifically, the UIA represents the first time a group of large public research universities has self-organized across state and conference lines for the specific purpose of scaling solutions to support student success and graduation. The UIA's vision is "that by piloting new interventions, sharing insights about their relative costs and effectiveness, and scaling those interventions that are successful, [they] will significantly increase the number of low-income Americans graduating with quality degrees and that, over time, [their] collaborative work will catalyze systemic changes in the entire higher education sector" (University Innovation Alliance, n.d.).

The UIA proposes to engage in three categories of work over the next three to five years: (1) identifying and verifying new solutions for student success; (2) scaling proven innovations to other interested institutions; and (3) communicating and distributing the experiences, results, and recommendations across the broader higher education landscape (University Innovation Alliance, n.d.). Managing this work is a multilayered team of representatives from each institution, led by the university presidents, and facilitated on a day-to-day basis by the UIA executive director. Each institution is represented by a college liaison who works with the primary faculty or staff who manage the interventions at their institutions, and by UIA Fellows. UIA Fellows are competitively selected professionals who support projects and assist with the exchange of ideas across UIA institutions. To effectively manage this partnership, UIA institutions have reached agreement on the governance model, the exchange of internal and external data, and specific innovations and priorities—including their first intervention, using predictive analytics.

As mentioned previously, another approach to collaboration is *collective impact*. As institutions continue to look for opportunistic ways to leverage the higher education ecosystem to address the needs of their students, specific components associated with collective impact can be found in examples of collaborative success. Specifically, collective impact is a collaborative, systemic, evidence-based approach to driving large-scale change across groups and organizations from multiple sectors (Kania & Kramer, 2011). As an approach, collective impact is useful for addressing problems or opportunities that are systemic, implicate a large target population and a significant number of actors, and extend beyond the capacity and resources of a single entity working in isolation. In some cases, foundations or other non-profit/government organizations provide the financial, technical support, and other resources needed to catalyze, sustain, or expand effective partnerships using a collective impact model. For example, Lumina Foundation's Community Partnership for Attainment seeks to mobilize entire communities by deepening the impact of cross-sector, place-based efforts to increase higher education attainment in cities across the United States. As part of this work, partner communities (numbering 75 as of December 2015) establish metropolitan regional partnerships based on active engagement and collaboration of political leadership, employers and business, higher education institutions, K–12 education, youth-serving organizations, local foundations and funders, college access networks, and faith-based and other community organizations. The work of partner communities rests on three central pillars: postsecondary attainment, equity, and (recognizing the vital dynamics of effective collaboration) partnership health. For more information on the work of the Community Partnerships for Attainment, visit www .luminafoundation.org.

Student-Centered Symbiosis in Support of Today's College Students

As we mentioned in chapter one, the profile of today's college student is vastly different from the frequently assumed archetype of the 18-year-old, nonminority student who lives in a dormitory and studies full-time in pursuit of a bachelor's degree. Racial diversity on college campuses has increased exponentially: from 1996 to 2010, the percentages of Hispanic and African-American college students increased 240 percent and 72 percent, respectively, compared to 11 percent for Whites (Lumina Foundation, n.d.). Erisman and Steele (2015) report that roughly 40 percent of today's undergraduates are older than 25, and adults age 50 and older represent roughly 20 percent of the considerable population of students who have some college credits but no degree. A large proportion of veterans and active military personnel are in the mix, as nearly 1.2 million veterans and 275,000 active military members sought postsecondary education benefits under the Post-9/11 Veterans Educational Assistance Act of 2008 between 2009 and 2013, and nearly 850,000 veterans, active military personnel, and dependents were reported as enrolled in colleges and universities for the 2012–13 academic year. Only 13 percent of American undergraduates live on campus, and 57 percent attend community colleges.

The unprecedented diversity of today's college students is accompanied by a set of similarly diverse challenges. Unsurprisingly, however, growing pressure to balance the costs of living with those of college is the most significant challenge for many students. Forty-seven percent of American undergraduates are financially independent, and 42 percent live near or below the poverty level (Lumina Foundation, n.d.). Significant numbers of undergraduates are balancing family responsibilities with their educational efforts, and many need to work while in school to make ends meet. Students of color are especially likely to be balancing parenting and college: 47 percent of African-American students, 42 percent of Native American students, and 25 percent of Hispanic students are raising children while in school (Lumina Foundation, n.d.); most, if not all of these students, too, must also work. The breadth and depth of these too-often-competing priorities establishes a gauntlet of financial, social, psychosocial, intellectual, and other challenges that significantly hinder the attainment prospects of the many undergraduates, who often face them with little institutional support. Recent studies reflect the toll of the challenge: only 11 percent of students living below the poverty level graduate within six years; 38 percent of students with additional financial, work, and family obligations leave school in their first year; and 53 percent of student parents leave college with no degree. Those who do complete are often saddled with debt, as 25 percent of bachelor's degree earners graduate with at least $24,000 in loan debt (Lumina Foundation, n.d.).

Erisman and Steele (2015) report that financial and family concerns also are top of mind for many veteran and active military students. Like other students, they often must balance work, family, and financial responsibilities, in addition to challenges unique to their military experience (such as navigating Veterans Administration benefits, dealing with mental or physical injuries or disabilities, pursuing college credit for their military training and experience, qualifying for in-state tuition, and fighting for policies that allow for tuition refunds and chances to complete courses that are interrupted by deployments). Those authors also cite research indicating that postsecondary institutions often are ill-equipped to meet the educational and career advising needs of students over 50, and that postsecondary programs for older adults often are aligned more toward personal enrichment than the workforce training that many of these students (who need or want to work longer than they had planned) actually need.

Since the beginning of the 21st century, increasing attention has been paid to the significant negative impact of issues affecting the success of specific student populations. Encouragingly, many institutions are demonstrating the opportunistic self-awareness necessary to acknowledge the impact of these issues; their obligation to provide enhanced (and some would say, nontraditional) student supports; and the necessity to reach beyond the campus boundaries to engage partners who can connect students with the resources they need to stabilize their situation and complete their studies. These partnerships and supports can include:

- Partnerships with local health, human and social service agencies, and Veterans Administration offices for on-campus access to veterans benefits and public benefits for nutrition assistance, health care, child care, and energy assistance

- Partnerships with state and local workforce investment boards that offer specialized funding and counseling resources for low-income students, veterans, and adult students who may be incumbent workers or changing/expanding their career training following years of experience in the labor market

- Partnerships with grocery stores, food pantries, and community organizations such as United Way to maintain on-campus food pantries

- Partnerships with financial institutions to provide financial coaching and access to resources such as Individual Development Accounts (IDAs)

- Partnerships with transportation authorities for low-or-no-cost bus passes for registered students

- Partnerships that provide on-campus access to legal assistance, car repair, and tax preparation services

An increasing number of American colleges and universities are using data-driven inquiry to determine the numbers of students in need of these services; some especially visionary institutions (such as Georgia State University) are working to isolate the impact of unmet financial need on completion by disaggregating retention and completion data based on student income and unmet need. This level of specificity enables the institution to deploy support resources (and report impact and return on investment data) in a much more strategic and effective way.

Chaplot, Cooper, Johnstone, & Karandjeff (2015) report just a few of the many campus partnerships taking place nationwide in support of students facing completion challenges due to unmet financial need. Examples of these partnerships include:

- Skyline College's partnership with the county human services agency to host a "CalFresh in a Day" event designed to help students apply and be approved for Supplemental Nutrition Assistance Program (SNAP) benefits within two hours

- The Benefits Access for College Completion (BACC) initiative, in which seven community and technical colleges collaborated with local public benefit agencies, national funders, and each other to increase completion rates by improving students' on-campus access to public benefits

- Central New Mexico Community College's renowned CNM Connect program, which embeds the core services of the typically community organization-led Working Families Success Network (WFSN) strategy into campus operations, thus providing on-campus access to financial literacy classes, personal finance, and tax preparation services, and access to public benefits and job and educational services

- A collaboration by six national funders, Achieving the Dream, nineteen community colleges, and higher education and community stakeholders in four states to scale the WFSN strategy into the Working Students Success Network

- The presence of Single Stop initiatives that provide on-campus access to public benefits, legal advice, financial counseling, tax preparation and counseling services, and other supports

These initiatives are in various stages of implementation, evaluation, and development; we list them to illustrate that institutional backing and resources for these types of student supports is ongoing, and aspiring student-ready colleges have a wide continuum of activities from which to choose. More information on these and other programs (and access to an institutional self-assessment that colleges can use to evaluate their programmatic supports for students with unmet financial need) is available at www.luminafoundation.org/bfa.

Student-ready colleges also have opportunities to explore partnerships aimed at better supporting veteran, military, and older adult students. While many of the issues affecting veteran and active military students are policy-oriented and resolved at the federal and/or state levels, Erisman and Steele (2015) report resources sponsored by veterans' affairs agencies (like the Minnesota Department of Veterans' Affairs, which offers a website, www.MyMilitaryEducation.org) can help student-ready colleges design programs and information strategies to improve support to these students. Institutional support for the unique supports needed for older students is also being demonstrated through campus-community collaborations such as those of the American Association for Community Colleges' "Plus 50" initiative, and the "Back to Work 50+" work led by the AARP Foundation.

Partnerships like these represent a significant departure from the traditional, "academic and tuition issues only" rules of engagement between the college campus and students. Institutions that engage students in these ways represent a vanguard that is willing to rewrite the old rules in the interest of scaffolding the financial and personal issues that too often represent the "lead dominoes" that—if compromised—begin the progressive toppling of the entire support structure for many of today's students.

Selecting Effective Partners

While there are several pathways to partnership, we note that many—if not most—effective partnerships in support of college students include several of the following factors:

1. *An appreciation of common work, strengths, and needs.*
   Effective partnerships begin and function as close to the core mission of each partner as possible. This priority should cause each partner to consider details including: the catchment area for each partner's activities, the target populations to be served (age, gender, race, income, family status, etc.), associated funding streams, active projects or priorities that incentivize or require work with partners matching the prospective partner's profile, and so on. Although the parties likely consider partnerships as an opportunity to meet needs, the "courtship" process should begin with an appreciation of the mission and work of each and the relative strengths that each can bring to the effort. The use of both quantitative and qualitative methods to illustrate their respective strengths, needs, and priorities

can help prospective partners clarify the form, function, and outcomes of the arrangement. Depending upon the service and the potential partner(s), the student-ready college should seek opportunities to make partnered services available in locations that are on or near campus.

2. *Overlapping accountabilities.* In addition to enabling a connection with an intrinsically motivated partner, connecting with partners with similar missions and goals enables student-ready colleges to share reciprocal accountability for reaching performance-based goals related to positive outcomes for the constituents who take advantage of their jointly offered services. For example, colleges with performance-based funding requirements and workforce investment boards with federal performance metrics for students receiving U.S. Department of Labor-funded services have overlapping target audiences and specific—but related—performance and data reporting requirements. These overlapping accountabilities should lead partners to seek, exchange, and report data associated with the delivery and outcomes of their respective services to students.

3. *Agreement on infrastructure.* The establishment of a supporting infrastructure for the partnership is essential in organizing and leading collaborations for impact; it involves the dedication of resources specifically focused on ongoing and regular support and communication to engage partners and to ensure the overall success of the partnership through careful planning and management. *It is also critical to determine at the outset which of the partners will serve as the "lead" in the partnership, and/or whether an intermediary will be needed to serve in that role.*

4. *A commitment to fairly share costs.* Negotiations around cost sharing will depend upon a number of factors, including: location of services and cost/in-kind value of space, amount of staff time needed for service delivery and support of the partnership, costs of materials and consumables (if any), and the use of grant resources (if any). The shared mission and potential benefits should help prospective partners recognize the potential value of working together and committing to bear appropriately proportional shares of the associated cost.

5. *Continuous communication.* Communication strengthens the relationship with the external partner and key constituent groups on campus. Engaged, regularly scheduled check-ins are vital to ensuring that student-ready colleges and their partners exchange pertinent data and other information on the volume, quality, and effectiveness of services being delivered. These check-ins also can provide opportunities for the partners to share updates on changing needs and priorities. Similarly, it is vital for the campus representatives in the partnership to regularly communicate with administration, faculty, staff, *and students* about the availability of services and their effectiveness (including "impact statistics" like numbers of students served and results obtained). In addition to increasing campus-wide awareness of and engagement in these services, these communications represent opportunities for partners to transmit vital messaging on the return on investment these services provide.

Questions to Ask as You Consider Partnerships to Support Student Success

1. Once you conduct quantitative and qualitative assessments of your campus' existing partnerships and a review of the other potential services partners might provide, what additional collaborations might your institution pursue?

2. What is the "climate" in and outside of your campus? In other words, what are the prevailing social, political, strategic, regulatory, financial, and cultural conditions that you should take into account when you:
   a. Select potential partners?
   b. Seek on-campus buy-in (if needed) to begin partnerships?
   c. Reach out to those partners?
   d. Design your commitments with those partners?
   e. Follow through on your respective commitments?

3. What will be the purpose of the relationship between your institution and the partner organization, and the specific roles and responsibilities of each party?

4. How will your institution communicate with the partner organization? Who will be your respective points of contact, and how often will you communicate?

5. Will the partner organization have a presence on campus?
   a. If so, how often will the organization come to campus?
   b. What type of arrangement makes the most sense, given the composition of your institution's student

population and the need you are trying to address through this partnership?

6. How will you ensure that eligible students know about the services available to them through this partnership, and that they are using these services?

7. How will you ensure that faculty and staff know about the services available to eligible students through this partnership, and that they are able to appropriately direct students to these services?

Conclusion

An objective view of the changing profile of American undergraduates makes clear that the already-challenging path to postsecondary attainment is becoming exponentially tougher for many students, for myriad reasons that originate away from—but ripple back into—the classroom. As we mentioned in chapter one, the history of higher education shows that the changing needs of student have always stretched the system, and the system has, in turn, adapted to accommodate the realities of the emergent student population. To enable the latest necessary adaptation, we call for all institutions to follow and expand the lead of those who have shown themselves willing to reconsider the traditional boundaries of "student support," examine their service offerings, and, where necessary, partner with external groups that can help them better support student success. These efforts are neither a luxury nor an imposition—they are the manifestation of an evolved survival instinct that ties institutional success and identity to the level of service provided to meet student needs.

·CHAPTER ONE·
In Search of the Student-Ready College

·CHAPTER TWO·
Leadership Values and Organizational Culture

·CHAPTER THREE·
Making Excellence Inclusive to Support Student Success

·CHAPTER FOUR·
Building Student Readiness through Effective Partnerships

CHAPTER FIVE
Demonstrating Belief in Students

CHAPTER·FIVE

Demonstrating Belief
in Students

Guiding Questions

- How can campus leaders keep both head and heart in the effort?

- How can leaders rely on empathy to guide institutional and community practice?

- How can leaders make the most of creative tensions in the community?

A student-ready campus genuinely believes in students. Leaders on a student-ready campus express genuine belief that all students have the capacity to learn. This concept appears to be straightforward and commonsensical, but it is actually quite difficult to achieve.

A belief in student talents and capacities is so strong on campuses that are ready for the students they have and the students they *will* have that it contributes in a meaningful and demonstrable way to campus values, identity, character, and ethos. What precisely does this mean? How can it be enacted? If we take a more searching look into the meaning of a belief in students, we can see why it is so difficult to achieve and in that way discover new avenues to get it done.

To believe deeply and genuinely in students means to believe that they can indeed *be* students. This is to say that they can learn—the most important objective of a college experience. It is to say that they can learn well and sufficiently.

It means that educators on the campus place a belief in students' talents and cognitive capacities ahead of, and in place of focusing on, any deficits that students may be perceived to carry. This vision of student capacity to learn or preparation to learn is inseparable from a vision of education for equity, social justice, and democratic well-being. It embraces all categories of difference that students embody. It incorporates an understanding of student potential within a learning-centered design for the institution—and a commitment to the institution in the context of its larger communities. As we say in chapter three, such a belief emerges in an array of actions that center on the assets all students bring to college and on pride in student achievement.

Belief in Student Capacity to Learn as a Genuine and Public Commitment

Those who work on campuses or with campus practitioners will note that many people across all types of institutions do believe that all students admitted to the institution have the capacity to learn—and specifically to learn well enough to complete the degree. Many educators are genuinely upbeat and hopeful and express their positive attitudes openly and freely. One of us recalls working at a racially and ethnically diverse institution that typically posts high ratings from students on National Survey of Student Engagement (NSSE) responses related to campus diversity. Students at this institution report that the community values diversity and that they appreciate the importance of that value as it contributes to their own learning. NSSE results on such campuses underscore something that people feel and express about the ethos of the campus: the value of diversity in its many dimensions and the capacities of all students to learn and contribute to the campus culture. The value that people throughout the campus community place on diversity can have a positive impact on pride in the community and the campus ethos. When this pride becomes a natural element of campus character, the effects can be palpable. There is no question that most members of a community that values diversity are proud that all students, and particularly students who historically have not been served well, are invited to thrive.

Evidence of such positive attitudes toward the learning of all students, across the full spectrum of difference, abounds in AAC&U's work. The spring 2015 and winter 2016 issues of *Diversity & Democracy* (Campbell, 2015; Campbell, 2016) carry many good examples. Titled *Gender Equity in Higher Education* and *The Equity Imperative*, the issues address race, ethnicity, gender, and sexual identity through an array of articles that make constructive recommendations for leadership to promote the flourishing of all students. The purpose of *Diversity & Democracy* is to share practical, evidence-based approaches and exemplary practices, supporting a vision of higher education that promotes student success and prepares students for socially responsible action. Reading *Diversity & Democracy* with a focus on making a campus ready for students can be helpful.

An artifact from an AAC&U project on a campus illustrates the value of perspective taking and belief in students' capacity to learn. The visual in Figure 5.1, developed by Sacramento State University (Hecsh, n.d.), exemplifies a positive view of student

Figure 5.1　Sacramento State: Graduation Initiative, General Education, and Closing the Achievement Gap

What?

Sacramento State Baccalaureate Learning Goals (BALGs)

Competence in the Disciplines *in at least one major field of study* and informed understandings of other fields, drawing on the knowledge and skills of disciplines outside the major.

Knowledge of Human Cultures and the Physical and Natural World. Focused by engagement with big questions, contemporary and enduring.

Intellectual and Practical Skills Practiced extensively, across the curriculum, in the context of progressively more challenging problems, projects, & standards for performance.

Personal and Social Responsibility: anchored through active involvement with diverse communities and real-world challenges.

Integrative Learning**, Including: *synthesis and advanced accomplishment* across general and specialized studies.

Demonstrated through application of knowledge, skills, and responsibilities to new settings and complex problems.

Who?

How?

High Impact Practices

Service Learning &
Community Engagement
FYE Experiences
Learning Communities
Capstone Experience

Common Intellectual
Experiences
Collaborative Assignments
Research and Inquiry
Internships, Study Abroad

Authentic Audience
Problem Solving

Program, Major, Course, Projects

Authentic Audience
Problem Solving

How Do We Get Better ?

DOMAINS:

VALUE RUBRICS:

Motivated & Sustained Learning

Lifelong Learning
Integrative Thinking
Intercultural Competence
Information Literacy

Communication

Oral Communication
Written Communication
Reading

Democratic Participation & Civic Engagement

Civic Engagement
Teamwork

Cognition

Critical Thinking
Creative Thinking
Inquiry and Analysis
Problem Solving
Ethical Reasoning
Quantitative Reasoning

Source: Hecsh (n.d.).

capacity that emerges across many projects on AAC&U member campuses. The visual centers on a photograph of a group of six diverse students, lying in a circle on a lawn, heads together, with smiling and open faces. This visual is placed at the center of a schematic design of general education, showing a plan for student learning outcomes and assessment. This visual representation of students does more than illustrate the diversity of the student body, in the way that view books typically do. It symbolically situates a positive regard for racially and ethnically diverse students at the center of the curriculum. It expresses Sacramento State's deep commitment to these students. It says loud and clear, "We believe these students can learn."

In a similar way, the recipients of the Aspen Prize—known for placing value on student learning and success—typically provide evidence that is not based solely on traditional markers of student success (such as graduation rates). The evidence demonstrates the institution's success in voicing a campus-wide ethos of belief in all students. Aspen awardees signal that their belief in students' capacity to learn is central to all that the institution does. In 2015, Western Kentucky Community and Technical College, in Paducah, Kentucky, was selected as a finalist with distinction for its success in creating a culture that supports college learning in a region where few people continue beyond high school. The effort to build and support a college-going culture is both campus and community wide. The whole community takes part in the work to believe in and support students. Speaking of the college, the Paducah Area Chamber of Commerce president observes, "The college is never satisfied with where they are. They're always striving to get to the next level, and they bring the community with them" (The Aspen Institute, 2015).

The Aspen Institute's *Crisis and Opportunity: Aligning the Community College Presidency with Student Success* (2013) has compiled research on truly effective presidencies. The first quality of leadership the report offers is this:

QUALITY 1: Deep Commitment to Student Access and Success.

A primary attribute of exceptional presidents is that they demonstrate a deep commitment to student access and success. While many who devote their careers to community colleges are concerned for the populations and missions their institutions serve, it is clear that some leaders, more than others, demonstrate a persistent, almost zealous drive to ensure student success while at the same time maintaining access for the broad range of students community colleges have traditionally served. For these presidents, this commitment is more than rhetoric; it is what drives them to become community college presidents and informs a great majority of their actions. Perhaps most important, a deep commitment to student access and success leads the most effective presidents to persist, over the long haul, in doing all the things needed to create lasting change on community college campuses. (p. 5)

This leadership quality carries an implicit belief in students' capacity to learn and leaders' capacity to create the conditions for learning. Such a commitment is especially important on less racially and ethnically diverse campuses, where experience tells us it may be harder to nurture and achieve. Yet we hasten to add that even diverse campus communities need to rely on the strength generated by their commitment to the full range of student diversity and pride in its achievement. This strength flows from a robust and fervent belief in students.

Challenges to Belief in Student Capacity to Learn

All campuses need this source of strength. Stereotyping doesn't dissolve and disappear easily in our society, even on highly diverse campuses. Social class bias and ethnic bias, two obvious examples of bias, intrude even there. Negative discrimination and backlash against change are possible to identify on any type of campus. Bias may also intrude as campus populations shift and change. Of late, with demographic changes becoming evident across the country, many campuses and communities have been rocked by abhorrent behavior expressed through acts of racially motivated hatred and gender-based violence. Given this reality, we want to remind readers that the strength to weather intergroup challenges and acts of discrimination and hatred emanates from a belief in students as learners—the heart and soul of the mission of any institution of higher learning that truly values excellence.

When student populations become more diverse on primarily white campuses, the belief system that ought to beat as if it is the heart of the campus may falter—as the observations and examples below will illustrate. Leaders on many campuses are indeed now paying attention to broader population trends in the United States and noting disparities in educational achievements among groups. There is no question of this awareness. But campus practitioners may place less value on changing student demographics, and on changing campus demographics more generally, than on concerns about overall enrollment trends, institutional rankings, or the financial viability of the institution. The value of demographic diversity may come across to outside observers and may be in fact considered by campus leaders as secondary to other considerations. All too often in our era of population change in the United States, campus community members may be inclined first to express their worries that today's students are not fully prepared for college. They may spring to these concerns before recognizing or acknowledging that the new campus diversity is good and welcome—and carries value in itself. As we visit campuses and listen to what people say about changing student demographics, we are accustomed to hearing remarks about the array of factors that have combined to make students less ready for college now than they were in the past.

We acknowledge that not all students are equally prepared for college. We will suggest later in this chapter some helpful designs for learning that address these differences in preparation. But first, we want to address negative perceptions held by faculty and administrators, the attitudes of campus leaders toward new majority students. These are the students we identify in Figure 1.2 who come from poor families, are racially and ethnically diverse, are older than traditional college age, are members of sexual minorities, have different learning needs, or are first in their families to attend college. Negative perceptions of the capacities of such students may shape campus discourse; they may be expressed as a kind of deficit-mindedness. This attitude can influence leaders and hence the organizational culture of the institution.

Truth to tell, we do hear expressions of deficit-mindedness as we visit primarily White institutions that are seeking to grow and/or diversify undergraduate enrollments. As the work to admit a more diverse student body proceeds, campus community members are likely to be noticing and discussing differences in their students compared with those admitted in the past. Unfortunately, all too often differences are perceived as deficiencies. Negative attitudes tend to build on one another to the point that faculty and administrators may express more negatives than positives when they talk about changing student populations. And deficit-mindedness is consequential. The stereotyping and associated acts of violence now reported in the news and popular press, echoing grimly and harking back to earlier eras, are cautionary reminders of what is at stake in the broader social context of the country when stereotyping reaches extremes. All campus leaders can address stereotyping where they see it. This is a particular opportunity for campus leaders who are White.

There is a connection between observations that students are not prepared for college and observations that some students are perceived to lack innate intelligence. As scholars such as Claude Steele, professor of psychology at Stanford University, have documented, the use of euphemisms and reliance on stereotypes tend to reinforce each other through a web of intersections, with complex effects on those who carry and those who bear the brunt of biases. Stereotyping and the complex web of interactions, perceptions, and behaviors it prompts can be extremely damaging and harmful to individuals and to the campus ethos.

Visitors to campus do often hear these worries and expressions of unexamined bias. The popular and trade press also pick them up. These popular perceptions matter. In 2014, for example, a letter to the *Washington Post* takes issue with the claim that 40 percent of students are unprepared for college. "Are American students grossly unprepared for college?" the letter asks, rhetorically (Burris, 2014). Community colleges, the author suggests, account for the larger share of the implied problem. In other words, according to the letter, the problem of unpreparedness is really a problem that affects community colleges more than it does the four-year sector. Unprepared students tend to choose community colleges rather than four-year institutions. Students are much stronger in the four-year sector—not "grossly unprepared." So the letter argues. But, we would observe in response, community colleges are the most diverse sector of higher education in terms of race, ethnicity, and range of income (Association of American Colleges and Universities, 2015). To say that the unprepared attend community colleges is as much as to imply, euphemistically, that the unprepared are poor and students of color. In fact, people who have had limited access to high-quality education will experience challenges of many kinds in college. But to shift the burden of blame for the problem to the students themselves and away from the social structures that support inequities is itself harmful. Through such a shift, the students become the problem. Negatives heap upon negatives, suggesting, in short, that there is something wrong with the students as potential learners. A similar shifting of blame appears in Supreme Court Justice Scalia's December 2015 comment: "While not posing a question directly, Scalia said he questioned whether admitting more black students would benefit them or the university. 'There are those who contend that it does not benefit African Americans to get into the University of Texas where they do not do well, as opposed to having them go to a less-advanced school, a slower-track school, where they do well,' Scalia said. He cited a brief that, he said, 'pointed out that most of the black scientists in this country don't come from schools like the University of Texas. They come from lesser schools' where they do not feel they're being pushed in classes 'that are too fast for them.'" (Savage, 2015).

It is not just in the popular press that one hears this refrain. It is echoed on campus after campus. We say this not to point fingers but to be frank and direct. *America's Unmet Promise* endeavors, with care, to lay out the facts and factors of inequities within social structures and institutions as a way to frame responsibility for education—to invite educators to understand disparities in education and to separate those conditions that harm students from the innate capacities that all students have to learn (Witham, Malcom-Piqueux, Dowd, & Bensimon, 2015).

We need to face and engage assumptions that lodge biases and to do that work in a productive and hopeful way. Our own campus visits to conduct workshops or facilitate projects have produced a set of cautionary examples—across institutional sectors. In truth, we have encountered a litany of negative descriptors attached to new majority students. For example, faculty and administrators frequently tell us that students know less and need more than they used to. They are not ready, we hear, for college. Even the locution "traditionally underserved" carries negative connotations, however mild. The language of underpreparedness and unpreparedness is euphemistic. It eclipses the belief that students can succeed in college. Once a negative mindset like this has taken hold in a community, one begins to hear far more about student deficits than about their capacities and talents.

How to address this all-too-common reality? It is indeed a leadership challenge. Leaders who believe in students can register and express positive and hopeful attitudes about students and their capacity to learn. They can prepare themselves to address discrimination and bias directly and thoughtfully. They can try their best to encourage civil dispute among diverse voices—in a positive way. A productive attitude here can lead to thoughtful, intentional, and direct communication. It can inform strategic and realistic action that improves institutional culture. It can help a person to express values and choose compassionate modes of communication. It can empower members of majority groups to speak up on behalf of persons in minority groups.

If you, as a leader, are hearing comments such as the following, we encourage you to take it as a leadership opportunity. We have heard all of these comments during our campus visits.

- The students were not well educated in high school.
- The problem is K–12.
- The community of origin was not college oriented.
- The grade school teachers and middle school teachers did not lay a good foundation.

- We have lowered our admissions standards.
- The home community lacks adequate health care for maternal and child well-being.
- The immigrant population from impoverished countries is not ready for college.
- The international students are culturally unprepared.
- Too many students require remediation.
- They don't read.
- The faculty cannot be expected to know how to teach such poorly prepared students.

Thinly disguised bias against new majority students in these negative examples resonates politically and is therefore difficult to touch. But deficit thinking like this need not predominate. It need not cloud our compassion. It need not preclude a positive outlook on the talents and capacities that all students bring. It need not displace tough-minded thinking and problem solving to address barriers to learning and success that so often cut off, marginalize, and harm the students we most urgently need to empower.

It is possible to upend or reverse the negative assumptions behind statements like these and to use the exercise to build leadership. One might think of it as an ideal opportunity to flip some orthodoxies, as Bansi Nagji and Helen Walters (2011) helpfully recommend. If you have never engaged in this kind of work, you might try. Basically, you create a safe space for discussion, identify closely held beliefs, treat the beliefs as morally neutral (whether they are or not), and then invert or reverse or deconstruct each belief. The results are likely to be illuminating.

If, for example, faculty and administrators point fingers at K–12 as the source of the problem of unpreparedness, one might consider how effectively the institution can address its own responsibilities for teacher education and community engagement with schools. If students don't read, educators might reconsider their responsibility for reading within their disciplines, using pedagogies such as Reading Apprenticeship (2015), which many educators find highly engaging.

New approaches to remediation are beginning to show evidence of a positive effect on learning outcomes and student success. The Tennessee Board of Regents, for example, is working on a system-wide plan to redesign remediation, based on a pilot study conducted by Austin Peay State University. Using a co-requisite model that is already posting evidence of success, the project is now being cited as a potential national model. Not only do all cohorts of students in remedial programs in the pilot study—cohorts defined by ACT scores—demonstrate significantly improved completion of credit-bearing courses in mathematics and English composition, but students in all ACT cohorts also show improvements on affective and noncognitive measures (T. Denley, e-mail correspondence, July 23, 2015). (For information on the Tennessee Board of Regents Co-Requisite Remediation Pilot Study, call on Tristan Denley, vice chancellor for academic affairs, Tennessee Board of Regents tristan.denley@tbr.edu, and see www.tbr.edu. Published outcomes are forthcoming.) It could likewise be significant on your campus to discuss emerging evidence from similar and related programs like the New Mathways project of the Charles A. Dana Center, University of Texas at Austin (2015). Across the country there are signs of breakthrough discoveries in developmental and remedial college learning that you do not want to miss. If you are a leader at a four-year institution, do not hesitate to turn to discoveries being made in the community college sector. You are almost certainly sharing the same students.

Finally, to flip one last sample orthodoxy, the wealth of cultural knowledge that diverse student populations bring to college can be a resource in and of itself. Culturally responsive teaching, pioneered by Geneva Gay (2010), can serve as a valuable resource for faculty.

A wealth of resources is available to support the work of making a campus ready for students. If you as a leader have the will and energy to make the case that all students you admit can learn sufficiently to complete a degree at your institution, you and your colleagues need not work with empty hands. Campus leaders can cultivate self-awareness and asset-minded capacities of leadership that support the best values of the community. They can find the tools they need. A community can choose to move in this direction. Leaders can be self-aware enough to use positive and affirming language about students even in cases when the situation calls for attention to something students need or lack—to use such language capably and sincerely, knowing that tools and frameworks exist, knowing that as leaders they are not alone.

We hasten to say that we are not calling for some new version of political correctness. A thoughtful, positive, self-aware discourse can be an intelligent and compassionate leadership strategy. It can be a subject of discussion and civil dispute in and of itself. As we have noted in chapter two, Alverno College has cultivated a community-wide belief in the capacities of women. They needed to reflect and act with a certain humility to achieve leadership of the kind that allowed them to pioneer development of an outcomes-directed curriculum. For example, at Alverno such endeavors as the Campus Civility Project invite the community to engage in perspective taking and to address social justice and historic inequities by being "willing to engage in conversations we are unsure of" (Alverno College, n.d.b, para 2). People used to say that Alverno could never serve as a model for other institutions because it is too small. Yet the practical and principled work with learning outcomes for student thriving that Alverno pioneered is indeed being scaled, as we will see, in other institutions.

The much larger Valencia College, which won the inaugural Aspen Prize for Community Colleges in 2011, has likewise cultivated a belief in student capacities. This belief emerges in important public places where one might not expect it. The human resources web pages at Valencia are replete with language indicating the institution's commitment to student readiness (Valencia College, 2015c). If you want a job at Valencia, you see these desired characteristics: "Individuals who not only believe in our students, but will help our students believe in themselves" (Valencia College, 2015a). What appears on the HR page reflects institution-wide goals. Valencia's strategic planning begins with a set of principles, identified as "Big Ideas." These principles are subject to campus-wide discussion. We do understand that discussions of this kind may become quite heated. The first challenging Big Idea at Valencia is this: "Anyone can learn anything under the right conditions" (Shugart, Phelps, Puyana, Romano, & Walter, n.d.).

As president, Sandy Shugart has chosen to launch a program of public discourse on values that make a student-ready college—values that may also be controversial. A president can make a necessary difference to such discussions. If a president leads and engages, other campus leaders will surely join.

We know from direct experience that a discussion of student capacity to learn can be difficult to manage and can take some bravery to sustain. But we also know it can be done. If you doubt your ability to conduct such a discussion, you may find resources for leading intergroup dialogue to be useful (Schoem & Hurtado, 2001).

We can think of many campuses where presidents have stepped forward to lead in this way. Freeman Hrabowski, of the University of Maryland Baltimore County, has made a famously lifelong commitment to inclusive leadership, starting with childhood activism in the Civil Rights movement (University of Maryland, Baltimore County, n.d.b). Dr. Hrabowski's leadership is dedicated to the values of civic mindedness and student readiness. But the institution of UMBC proclaims itself to be more than the president's commitments. The UMBC community demonstrates how the ethos of the institution expresses shared values that are dedicated to the thriving and empowerment of undergraduates. Among innovations at UMBC, the BreakingGround initiative uses an array of approaches to support students, faculty, and staff as they participate in the life of the campus, in Baltimore, and in the world beyond (Hoffman, Berger, & Bickel, 2015). The BreakingGround blog shows eloquently how to empower undergraduates through their own learning. "Dig In," the blog's banner proclaims; "Shape Your World." (University of Maryland, Baltimore County, n.d.a). Theophilus Aluko (2015), mechanical engineering student, class of 2016, blogs about his experience, "seeing how students are able to impact meaningful change to create the world they envision. Like someone from my church would say: 'The problem that annoys you may be the very reason you're here'" (para. 5).

A Learning-Centered Campus Designed for All Students to Flourish

Having made the claim that all students can learn and that a belief in students can fuel change, we return to the concept of the learning-centered institution. A belief in student capacity to learn and the robust structures of a learning-centered experience in the curriculum and co-curriculum can produce an effective mission-driven and visionary engine for leadership. We can cite a number of resilient examples. Over many years, Indiana University Purdue University Indianapolis (IUPUI) has pioneered in the use of learning outcomes. IUPUI has made this effort based on commitment to student success, particularly for the diverse array of students who attend urban public universities. The Principles of Undergraduate Learning at IUPUI have gone through stages and generations of change and application since the 1990s. They stand as testimonial that a large and diverse research university can keep student learning at the center of campus values. Portland State University, likewise a pioneer in general education as engaged entrée to college, takes pride in their decades of work to bring the first-year experience to life for all students. The University Studies Program at Portland State, launched in the early 1990s, takes pride as it speaks in plain and direct language to undergraduates: "Our innovative, award-winning general education program teaches you how to learn" (Portland State University, 2015). The examples of program activities in general education include lively experiential work beyond the classroom, emphasizing community-based and environmental service and creative inquiry.

Examples of intentional leadership centered on student learning and belief in student capacities may be found in many institutions across the country. Eastern Connecticut State University President Elsa Núñez articulates a thoughtful leadership philosophy for her campus that says, "This is a learning-centered institution that believes in students!" Her leadership choices are anchored in commitment to students, a commitment moved energetically into action:

> When new students arrive on Eastern's campus, we want them to feel at home, so we engage them in a number of ways. Our approach with freshmen ranges from high-touch personal interactions to exciting events to support systems and programs. One freshman might get invited out for lunch by their resident assistant. Others will enjoy the opportunity to join a club, intramural team, or other organization during the student activity fair held during the first week of school. And behind the scenes, a sophisticated early warning system helps ensure that at-risk students are quickly identified and supported. The goal is to engage freshmen quickly while giving them the immediate feeling that they belong to a special community. We want Eastern students

to become confident in their skills and comfortable in their skins—everything we do on campus serves to make that happen. (personal communication, August 20, 2015)

President José Antonio Bowen is leading Goucher College to help students prepare for "the unknown" in their lives ahead through active learning and innovation, pushing the limits of college admissions practices to attract diverse student talent (Simon, 2014). President Brian Murphy, De Anza College, Cupertino, California, has built his leadership on a profound belief in the societal importance of community college student success. Founder of the Democracy Commitment, Murphy launched a national organization dedicated to civic engagement and renewal:

> The Democracy Commitment (TDC) is a national initiative providing a platform for development and expansion of community college programs, projects and curricula aiming at engaging students in civic learning and democratic practice across the country. Our goal is that every graduate of an American community college has had an education in democracy. This includes all of our students, whether they aim to transfer to university, achieve an associate degree or obtain a certificate. (The Democracy Commitment, n.d.)

Student-ready leaders know that senior administrators, including presidents, need to express belief in students and be bold in stating that students can flourish and find life purpose. But wise leaders also recognize that they cannot alone achieve change that permeates the culture, the kind of eco-systemic change we have been discussing. The effort demands widely shared and self-aware leadership.

Guiding Questions for All Leaders

- What language predominates in campus discussions of students and their capacity to learn? Is the language compassionate? Is it frank and genuine? Is it consistently hopeful?

- What rhetorical strategies do campus leaders consider when they talk about students? Has the concept of the student-ready campus and belief in student capacity been a topic of discussion across units? Has it been a goal for collaborative cross-functional effort?

- What opportunities do educators have to engage in honest and open discourse and civil disagreement about the talents and capacities of students? What experience with intergroup dialogue has the campus gained? (A useful list of research resources on intergroup dialogue may be found on the Syracuse University website at http:// intergroupdialogue.syr.edu/research/.)

- Does your campus define student success in terms of achievement of learning outcomes? Does success include other indicators of student flourishing, including affective and noncognitive growth? How much do you know about the ways your students are learning beyond the typical indicators of achievement such as graduation rates, time to degree, and grade point averages?

- How would you describe the ethos of your campus? Is the campus welcoming of difference across and among student populations? Across and among faculty and staff populations? What might you do to encourage discussion of campus ethos?

- How might you flip some orthodoxies to bring serious and consequential discussions into the light of day?

Conclusion

Student-ready leaders will find what effective leaders have long known: a top-down expression of belief in students, necessary as it is, cannot in and of itself be sufficient. A student-ready campus as a whole makes belief in students intentional, an inviting expectation of everyone who works there—from the ground up, and from the top down, keeping an eye on the horizon and welcoming new ideas from beyond the institution. They will recognize that it takes both compassion and bravery to work with tensions in the community.

CONCLUSION

Generations do not cease to be born, and we are responsible
to them because we are the only witnesses they have.

—James Baldwin, *The Fire Next Time* (1963)

Becoming a *Student-Ready College* has given the authors a chance to stretch our individual and collective imaginations. We began the adventure of writing this book because we wanted to serve the values and commitments that have animated our careers. The book gave us a chance to concentrate on a shared vision of the student-ready college and to approach that vision from our own different vantage points and bases of experience in work with and for higher education. We wanted to share a vision and use it to invite colleagues to see anew. We hope that you, the reader, have indeed seen something different and felt both challenged and refreshed.

Vision alone, we know, is not sufficient. Above all, we intend to be pragmatic in making recommendations for change on campuses. Many of us dedicate our lives to higher education, trying our best to reform, redesign, and renew for the sake of our beautiful students, for the benefit and resilience of our ever-evolving pluralistic democracy. Change often does seem incremental, and sometimes we lose ground. Despite these challenges, we are writing a hopeful book. Hope keeps us going, and it is a grounded and serious hope. We want to keep our eyes on ideals and greater goals, in sight, in mind and heart, as we anchor those higher concepts in the ground of ordinary work, in the day-to-day realities of things as they are on campuses.

We continue to hope that what ought to be actually *can* be. Student-ready campuses are achievable. We are absolutely convinced that *all students* can thrive in such institutions. The way to change can indeed follow the will to change. Although it never is easy, change that works has to be guided by profoundly important values and then turned to action. We believe collectively that colleges and universities can remake themselves as strong and nurturing communities for all the students they now have and the students of the future.

Motivation to write this book came from many sources. A strong point of convergence arose in our shared insight that educators need to address our own mythmaking. We do have our own set of higher education myths and orthodoxies. Acknowledging that failing is helpful. We go nowhere unless we scrutinize our unexamined beliefs, underscore them, interrogate them, fearlessly go after them for deeper insights and practical action. We all knew when we started the book that many educators pine for the golden age of American higher education, the days when things were different. At the same time, we all agreed that the golden age of American higher education, when every student came well prepared for college, is a myth—always has been a myth. The United States has never experienced a time like that. So first, we wanted, as responsible educators, to call out that myth and show it for what it is.

But we were determined to call it out compassionately and continue to work forward with hope and good ideas.

In closing the book, we want first to converge on the book's key idea. What educators call the "college-ready" student was an image and an identity that could be flipped or inverted in order to convey a powerful message. Instead of striving and struggling to make students ready for college, we could work hard, as a society and locally, on individual campuses, to make college ready for students. We realized that we could look at the constituent elements of campus communities, the people and the structures, and change perspective by using a new lens—a student-ready lens, so to speak. We thought that a powerful new perspective truly could help people see anew. Students and faculty and institutions look different through a student-ready lens. Governance looks different. Community engagement looks different. Educator responsibilities look different.

Having figured out, first, that we could invite readers—educators—to see anew, having invited our readers to do just that, we wanted to concentrate on action. Critically important action needs to address the talents and assets all students bring to college. We cannot say this too often or too strongly. Educators need to be reminded—we *all* need to be reminded—of the essential value of a positive view of all students, of the need to see past and put aside perceptions of student deficits. For many people this is a new mindset. Once an educator sees students in a new way, other vistas open and new actions become attractive and feasible. Subsequent discoveries about one's own personal and institutional responsibility and accountability are likely to follow. See students differently, and one sees a campus community differently. One's own place in that community will shift. This is a new way to see a campus and then to invite educators to become leaders and to take action. Many of the recommendations we make proceed from the vision of all students as ready for college, no matter their pathway to our doors.

Second, we realized that we needed to take a holistic and ecological approach to the concept of making college communities ready for students. The idea of interconnection can help people see how systems and structures work. Using an organic, life-affirming set of metaphors for change worked well for us. Campuses do form a network of life within and beyond their communities. Educators can and should act on that knowledge. This awareness led to our guiding definition: "A student-ready college is one that strategically and holistically advances student success, and works tirelessly in its pursuits to educate ALL students for civic and economic participation in a global, interconnected society."

We also were reminded that there could be power inherent in the very tensions we wanted to share. There is tension between taking responsibility for student flourishing in our time and the pull of traditional practices and ways of institutions. As we have observed, beyond the conventional parameters of what is already known and the grasp of questions that have already been answered, beyond the familiar conventions and traditions associated with serving yesterday's students, we urge readers to embrace the new realities of the higher education ecosystem in our time and for the future.

Third, we acknowledge that the scope of such change is enormous. Experience has taught us in sometimes stunning ways. Yet we grasp hope firmly. We see the challenges and hope we know them for what they are. Many are indeed intractable. It is one thing to have the vision and another to put it to work. Recognizing that campuses have the will, we wonder and cannot quite shake the concern that they might not find the way. Yet there is no perfect time. Waiting for a better time rarely helps. Finding strength in some of the practices and structures we have available right now, meeting educators where they are right now—because we can't afford to wait—became an insight that guided our thinking. To meet the enormous challenge of change, we began to look for capacities on campuses and in communities that often are overlooked, including the potential that grows on a campus where every employee is an educator.

There are steps that campus leaders can take right now—actions and decisions that are different. For example, leaders can think critically about the need to cultivate new and different attitudes. It is worth talking about campus values and beliefs, about attitudes toward change, about unexamined assumptions and biases. From time to time, reflection on campus ethos is helpful and can lead to action. Leaders can invite colleagues to be compassionate, self-reflective, and empathetic, to be creative, nimble, and dynamic. It is hard to imagine a college that doesn't include people who share these attitudes and values—along with valuing hopes for change.

Sometimes it is helpful to identify a finite and concrete step to take. We hope that we have offered a number of examples. For instance, leaders might recognize the compelling need to change the traditional rules of engagement based on academic-and-tuition-only policies for students. Students as human beings need and deserve much more. They are hungry, often literally, for more.

And campuses aren't isolated and solitary. They exist in communities. There is great potential inherent in the local and larger communities in which colleges exist. It can be most helpful to invite creative thinking to guide institutions as they work with external partners to provide holistic student supports and pathways for learning.

If we had to identify one shared worry as we close the book, it would be the risk in all pragmatic calls for change. Pragmatism is itself a philosophy that seeks connection and commerce between idea and action. The student-ready college is one thing as an idea or ideal. It is another thing on the ground. We acknowledge this concern: Without clearly defined action steps, "becoming a student-ready college" could become one of the many catch phrases in higher education that everyone agrees with, but no one really understands.

This book asks for serious and consequential work. If we do not change higher education, if we do not steadfastly and courageously try, we see enormous risks ahead. The convergent forces of demographic, economic, environmental, and techno-logical change could have catastrophic effects on 21st-century students. Despite the devastating loss of talent and loss of opportunity among young people going on right now, we see astonishing potential to be released. An unclouded view of the way campuses fail students can motivate. Our book looks resolutely beyond the clouds. We believe that a vision and a whole host of practices are right before us, showing us how to make ourselves and our institutions ready for students.

REFERENCES

Aluko, T. (2015, June 16). *The very reason you are here*. Retrieved from UMBC BreakingGround at Wordpress: https://umbcbreakingground.wordpress.com/2015/06/16/the-very-reason-you-are-here/

Alverno College. (1994; 2001). *Ability-based learning program: The history major*. Milwaukee, WI: Alverno College Institute.

Alverno College. (n.d.a). *Admissions*. Retrieved from Alverno College: http://www.alverno.edu/admissions/#graduate

Alverno College. (n.d.b). *Civility project*. Retrieved from Alverno College: http://www.alverno.edu/campuslife/civilityproject/

Andrews, J. (2006). How we can resist corporatization. *Academe, 92*(3), 16–19. Retrieved from http://www.jstor.org/stable/40252920

The Aspen Institute. (2013). *Crisis and opportunity: Aligning the community college presidency with student success*. Washington, DC: Author. Retrieved from http://www.aspeninstitute.org/sites/default/files/content/docs/pubs/CEP_Final_Report.pdf

The Aspen Institute. (2015). *The 2015 Aspen Prize.* Washington, DC: Author. Retrieved from http://www .aspeninstitute.org/sites/default/files/content/docs/pubs/ 2015AspenPrizePublication.pdf

Association of American Colleges and Universities. (n.d.a). *Essential learning outcomes.* Retrieved from http://www.aacu .org/leap/essential-learning-outcomes

Association of American Colleges and Universities. (n.d.b). *Making excellence inclusive.* Retrieved from http://www.aacu .org/making-excellence-inclusive

Association of American Colleges and Universities. (n.d.c). *Intercultural knowledge and competence VALUE rubric.* Retrieved from https://www.aacu.org/value/rubrics/ intercultural-knowledge

Association of American Colleges and Universities. (2007). *College learning for the new global century: A report from the national leadership council for liberal education & America's promise.* Washington, DC: Author. Retrieved from http://www .aacu.org/sites/default/files/files/LEAP/GlobalCentury_final .pdf

Association of American Colleges and Universities. (2012, January/February). *Using LEAP to connect work and learning: The university center at the University of Wisconsin–Whitewater.* Retrieved from http://www.aacu.org/campus-model/using- leap-connect-work-and-learning-university-center-university- wisconsin%E2%80%93whitewater

Association of American Colleges and Universities. (2015). *Committing to equity and inclusive excellence: A campus guide for self-study and planning*. Washington, DC: Author.

Baum, S., Ma, J., & Payea, K. (2013). *Education pays 2013: The benefits of higher education for individuals and society*. Washington, DC: College Board. Retrieved from http://trends .collegeboard.org/sites/default/files/education-pays-2013-full-report.pdf

Bean, J. P. (1983). The application of a model of turnover in work organizations to the student attrition process. *Review of Higher Education, 6*, 129–148.

Benjamin, D., Chambers, S., & Reiterman, G. (1993). A focus on American Indian college persistence. *Journal of American Indian Education, 32*(2), 24–40.

Bensimon, E. M., & Malcom, L. (Eds.). (2012). *Confronting equity issues on campus: Implementing the equity scorecard in theory and practice*. Sterling, VA: Stylus Publishing.

Berger, J. B. (2000). Optimizing capital, social reproduction, and undergraduate persistence. In John Braxton (Ed.), *Reworking the student departure puzzle* (pp. 95–124). Nashville, TN: Vanderbilt University Press.

Berger, J. B., & Braxton, J. M. (1998). Revising Tinto's interactionalist theory of student departure through theory elaboration: examining the role of organizational attributes in the persistence process. *Research in Higher Education, 39*(2), 103–119.

Braskamp, L. A., Trautvetter, C. L., & Ward, K. (2006). *Putting students first: How colleges develop students purposefully*. San Francisco, CA: Jossey-Bass.

Braxton, J. M. (2000). Reinvigorating theory and research on the departure puzzle. In John Braxton (Ed.), *Reworking the student departure puzzle* (pp. 257–274). Nashville, TN: Vanderbilt University Press.

Bronfenbrenner, U. (2005). *Making human beings human: Bioecological perspectives on human development*. Thousand Oaks, CA: SAGE.

Brookdale Community College. (2013). *Vision, mission and values*. Retrieved from http://www.brookdalecc.edu/about/vision-mission-values/

Bryk, A. S., Gomez, L. M., and Grunow, A. (2010). *Getting ideas into action: Building networked improvement communities in education*. Stanford, CA: Carnegie Foundation for the Advancement of Teaching. Retrieved from http://www.carnegiefoundation.org/resources/publications/getting-ideas-action-building-networked-improvement-communities-education/

Bullard, D. (2007). *Academic capitalism in the social sciences: Faculty responses to the entrepreneurial university*. University of South Florida Scholar Commons. Retrieved from http://scholarcommons.usf.edu/cgi/viewcontent.cgi?article=1646&context=etd

Burris, C. (2014, March 17). Are American students grossly unprepared for college? *The Washington Post*. Retrieved from http://www.washingtonpost.com/blogs/answer-sheet/wp/2014/03/17/are-american-students-grossly-unprepared-for-college/

Busteed, B. (2015, June 12). *The two most important questions for graduates*. Gallup. Retrieved from http://www.gallup.com/ opinion/gallup/183599/two-important-questions-graduates .aspx?utm_source=CATEGORY_EDUCATION&utm_ medium=topic&utm_campaign=tiles

California State University, Fullerton. (n.d.a). *California State University, Fullerton strategic plan 2013–2018*. Retrieved from http://planning.fullerton.edu/_resources/pdf/CSUF-Strategic-Plan.pdf

California State University, Fullerton. (n.d.b). *Mission statement*. Retrieved from http://webcert.fullerton.edu/aboutcsuf/ mission.asp

Callejo Perez, D. M., & Ode, J. (Eds.). (2013). *The stewardship of higher education: Re-imagining the role of education and wellness on community impact*. Rotterdam: Sense Publishers.

Calderón, J. Z., & Pollack, S. (2015, Summer). Weaving together career and civic commitments for social change (S. J. Carey, Ed.). *Peer Review, 17*(3).

Campbell, K. P. (Ed.). (2015, Spring). *Diversity & Democracy: Gender Equity in Higher Education, 18*(2).

Campbell, K.P. (Ed). 2016, Winter). *Diversity & Democracy: The Equity Imperative, 19*(1).

Centre College. (2014, September). *Faculty handbook*. Retrieved from http://www.centre.edu/wp-content/uploads/ 2014/09/handbook_faculty.pdf

Chaplot, P., Cooper, D., Johnstone, R., & Karandjeff, K. (2015). *Beyond financial aid: How colleges can strengthen the financial stability of low-income students and improve outcomes.* Indianapolis, IN: Lumina Foundation. Retrieved from http://www.luminafoundation.org/files/publications/BFA/Beyond.Financial.Aid.pdf

The Charles A. Dana Center, University of Texas at Austin. (2015). *The new mathways project.* Retrieved from http://www.utdanacenter.org/higher-education/new-mathways-project/

Colter, J. (2013, October 31). Positive energy and enthusiasm soar as PGCC staff and faculty members engage in college enrichment day. Prince George's Community College. Retrieved from https://www.pgcc.edu/News_Stories/Positive_Energy_and_Enthusiasm_Soar_as_PGCC_Staff_and_Faculty_Members_Engage_in_College_Enrichment_Day.aspx

Complete College America. (2014, December). *Four-year myth: Make college more affordable. Restore the promise of graduating on time.* Indianapolis, IN: Author. Retrieved from http://completecollege.org/wp-content/uploads/2014/11/4-Year-Myth.pdf

Côte, J., & Allahar, A. (2011). *Lowering higher education: The rise of corporate universities and the fall of liberal education.* Toronto, ON: University of Toronto Press.

The Delphi Project on the Changing Faculty and Student Success. (2014). *The Delphi Project on the Changing Faculty and Student Success.* Pullias Center for Higher Education. Retrieved from http://thechangingfaculty.org/

The Democracy Commitment. (n.d.) *The initiative.* Retrieved from http://thedemocracycommitment.org/about-us/the-initiative/

Dolinsky, R., Ferren, A., & McCambly, H. (2015, Fall/Winer). Collaborative, faculty-led efforts for sustainable change (S. J. Carey, Ed.). *Peer Review, 16/17*(4/1). Retrieved from http://www.aacu.org/peerreview/2014–2015/fall-winter/research

Engelmann, D. (2007, August 14). Assessment from the ground up. Inside Higher Ed. Retrieved from https://www.insidehighered.com/views/2007/08/14/engelmann

Erisman, W., & Steele, P. (2015). Adult college completion in the 21st century: What we know and what we don't. Washington, DC: Higher Ed Insight. Retrieved from http://www.adultcollegecompletion.org/sites/files/documents/images/Adult%20College%20Completion%20in%20the%2021st%20Century.pdf

Felten, P., Bauman, H.-D. L., Kheriaty, A., Taylor, E., & Palmer, P. J. (2013). *Transformative conversations: A guide to mentoring communities among colleagues in higher education.* San Francisco, CA: Jossey-Bass.

Finley, A., & McNair, T. (2013). *Assessing underserved students' engagement in high-impact practices.* Washington, DC: Association of American Colleges and Universities.

Fry, C. L. (Ed.). (2014). *Achieving systemic change: A sourcebook for advancing and funding undergraduate STEM education.* Washington, DC: Association of American Colleges and Universities. Retrieved from https://www.aacu.org/sites/default/files/files/publications/E-PKALSourcebook.pdf

Gasman, M. (2008). *Historically black colleges and universities: Triumphs, troubles, and taboos.* New York, NY: Palgrave Macmillan.

Gaston, P. L., & Gaff, J. G. (2009). *Revising general education—and avoiding the potholes: A guide for curricular change*. Washington, DC: Association of American Colleges and Universities.

Gay, G. (2010). *Culturally responsive teaching: Theory, research, and practice* (2nd ed.). New York, NY: Teachers College Press.

Georgetown University. (n.d.). *Designing the futures(s) of the university*. Retrieved from https://futures.georgetown.edu/

Giroux, H. (2014). *Neoliberalism's war on higher education*. Chicago, IL: Haymarket Books.

Goodman, M., Sands, A., & Coley, R. (2015). America's skills challenge: Millennials and the future. Princeton, NJ: Center for Research on Human Capital and Education, Educational Testing Service. Retrieved from http://www.ets.org/s/research/30079/asc-millennials-and-the-future.pdf

Hamilton, N. W., & Gaff, J. G. (2009). *The future of the professoriate: Academic freedom, peer review, and shared governance*. Washington, DC: Association of American Colleges and Universities.

Hart Research Associates. (2015, November). *Bringing equity and quality learning together: Institutional priorities for tracking and advancing underserved students' success*. Retrieved from https://www.aacu.org/sites/default/files/files/LEAP/2015AACUEquityReport.pdf

Harvey, V. S. (2007). *Schoolwide methods for fostering resiliency*. National Association of Secondary School Principals. Retrieved from http://www.nasponline.org/resources/principals/schoolresiliency.pdf

Hecsh, J. (n.d.). *Connecting the dots between learning goals, high-impact practices and assessment.* AAC&U LEAP Toolkit. Retrieved from http://leap.aacu.org/toolkit/wp-content/uploads/2011/11/Connecting_the_Dots_SacSt.pdf

Hensel, N. H., Hunnicutt, L., & Salomon, D. A. (Eds.). (2015). *Redefining the paradigm: Faculty models to support student learning.* The New American Colleges and Universities. Retrieved from http://www.newamericancolleges.org/Monograph/redef1n1_issue_low.pdf

Hoffman, D., Berger, C., & Bickel, B. (2015, Winter). Democratic agency and the visionary's dilemma (K. P. Campbell, Ed.). *Diversity and Democracy: Publicly Engaged Scholarship and Teaching, 18*(1). Retrieved from http://www.aacu.org/diversitydemocracy/2015/winter/hoffman

Ignash, J. M. (1997). Who should provide postsecondary remedial developmental education? In J. M. Ignash (Ed.), *Implementing effective policies for remedial and developmental education.* New Directions for Community Colleges, no. 100 (pp. 5–20). San Francisco, CA: Jossey-Bass.

Imagining America. (n.d.). Retrieved from http://imaginingamerica.org/

Institute for Higher Education Policy. (1998). *College remediation: What it is, what it costs, and what's at stake.* Washington, DC: Author.

Institute for Higher Education Policy. (2013, January). *Supporting men of color along the educational pipeline: Research and practice.* Washington, DC: Author. Retrieved from http://www.ihep.org/sites/default/files/uploads/docs/pubs/pcn_supportingmenofcolor.pdf. Reprinted from Literacy Connects.

Kania, J., & Kramer, M. (2011, Winter). Collective impact. *Stanford Social Innovation Review*. Retrieved from http://ssir .org/articles/entry/collective_impact

Kean, R. C., Mitchell, N. D., & Wilson, D. E. (2008, Fall). Toward intentionality and transparency: Analysis and reflection on the process of general education reform (S. J. Carey, Ed.). *Peer Review*, *10*(8). Retrieved from http://www.aacu.org/ sites/default/files/files/peerreview/PRFall08.pdf

Kegan, R., & Lahey, L. L. (2009). *Immunity to change: How to overcome it and unlock the potential in yourself and your organization*. Boston: Harvard Business Press.

Kezar, A. (2015). *Scaling and sustaining change and innovation: Lessons learned from the Teagle Foundation's "Faculty Work and Student Learning" initiative*. New York, NY: The Teagle Foundation. Retrieved from http://www .teaglefoundation.org/getmedia/f5560934-c4db-42e3-8e52- 439bd7aa82f6/Kezar-Sustaining-Change

Kezar, A. J., & Lester, J. (2009). *Organizing higher education for collaboration: A guide for campus leaders*. San Francisco, CA: Jossey-Bass.

Kirwan Institute for the Study of Race and Ethnicity. (2015). *Understanding implicit bias*. Retrieved from http:// kirwaninstitute.osu.edu/research/understanding-implicit- bias/

Kramer, G. L., & Gardner, J. N. (2007). *Fostering student success in the campus community*. San Francisco, CA: Jossey-Bass.

Kucia, J. F., & Gravett, L. S. (2014). *Leadership in balance: New habits of the mind*. New York, NY: Palgrave Macmillan.

Kuh, G. D. (2008). *High-impact educational practices: What they are, who has access to them, and why they matter*. Washington, DC: Association of American Colleges and Universities.

Kuh, G. D., & O'Donnell, K. (2013). *Ensuring quality & taking high-impact practices to scale*. Washington, DC: Association of American Colleges and Universities.

Lave, J., & Wenger, E. (1991). *Situated learning: Legitimate peripheral participation*. Cambridge: Cambridge University Press.

Lerner, G. L., & Brand, B. (2006). *The college ladder: Linking secondary and postsecondary education for success for all students*. Washington, DC: American Youth Policy Forum. Retrieved from http://www.aypf.org/publications/ The%20College%20Ladder/TheCollegeLadderlinking secondaryandpostsecondaryeducation.pdf

Lumina Foundation. (n.d.). *Statistics*. Retrieved from https:// www.luminafoundation.org/todays-student-statistics

Lumina Foundation. (2014). Higher education land- scape. Lumina Foundation: Indianapolis.

Lumina Foundation. (2015a, June). The importance of partnerships. *Report of Organizational Performance and Evaluation—ROPE*, 1–4.

Lumina Foundation. (2015b). Partnerships, networks, collabo- ratives! Oh my! Unpublished raw data.

Lumina Foundation. (2015c). *A stronger nation through higher education: Ten-year time horizon brings Goal 2025 into sharp focus*. Indianapolis: Author. Retrieved from http://strongernation.luminafoundation.org/report/

Manning, K. (2013). *Organizational theory in higher education*. New York, NY: Routledge.

McClure, L., Yonezawa, S., & Jones, M. (June, 2010). *Personalization and caring relationships with adults in urban high school: Is there a relationship with academic achievement? California Education Supports Project* Brief #5. Retrieved from https://create.ucsd.edu/_files/publications/CESP_policybrief5_UCSD.pdf

Mentkowski, M. (2000). *Learning that lasts: Integrating learning, development, and performance in college and beyond*. San Francisco, CA: Jossey-Bass.

Miller, A., Valle, K., Engle, J., & Cooper, M. (2014, December). *Access to attainment: An access agenda for 21st century college students*. Washington, DC: Institute for Higher Education Policy. Retrieved from http://www.ihep.org/sites/default/files/uploads/docs/pubs/ihep_access-attainment_report_layout_rd5_web.pdf

Nagji, B., & Walters, H. (2011, Fall). Flipping orthodoxies: Overcoming insidious obstacles to innovation. *Rotman Magazine*, 60–65.

National Center for Education Statistics. (2014). *Digest of education statistics: 2014*. Washington, DC: Author. Retrieved from https://nces.ed.gov/programs/digest/d14/tables/dt14_303.10.asp?current=yes

O'Brien, J., Littlefield, J., & Goddard-Truitt, V. (2013). A matter of leadership: Connecting a grantmaker's investments in collaborative leadership development to community results. *The Foundation Review, 5*(1), 26–41.

Park, T. (2012). Academic capitalism and its impact on the American professoriate. *Journal of the Professoriate, 6*(1), 84–99.

Pascarella, E. T. (1985). College environmental influences on learning and cognitive development: A critical review and synthesis. In J. C. Smart (Ed.), *Higher education: Handbook of theory and research* (Vol. 4, pp. 1–61). New York, NY: Agathon.

Pew Research Center. (2013, June 10). *A survey of LGBT Americans: Attitudes, experiences and values in changing times.* Retrieved from http://www.pewsocialtrends.org/2013/06/13/a-survey-of-lgbt-americans/

Professional and Organizational Development (POD) Network. (2007–2015). Retrieved from http://podnetwork.org/

Portland State University. (2015). *University studies.* Retrieved from https://www.pdx.edu/unst/

Reading Apprenticeship at WestEd. (2015). Retrieved from readingapprenticeship.org

Rochester Institute of Technology. (n.d.). *2015–2025 strategic plan.* Retrieved from https://www.rit.edu/president/strategicplan2025/dimension5.html

Savage, D. (2015, December 10). Justice Scalia under fire for race comments during affirmative action argument. *Los Angeles Times.* Retrieved from http://www.latimes.com/nation/la-na-scalia-race-20151210-story.html

Schoem, D., & Hurtado, S. (2001). *Intergroup dialogue: Deliberative democracy in school, college, community, and workplace.* Ann Arbor, MI: University of Michigan Press.

Schreiner, C. (2015). Student workers and staff supervisor. University of Wisconsin-Whitewater.

Schroeder, C. (2010). *Coming in from the margins: Faculty development's emerging organizational development role in institutional change.* Herndon, VA: Stylus Publishing, LLC.

Shugart, S. C., Phelps, J., Puyana, A., Romano, J., & Walter, K. (n.d.). *Valencia's big ideas: Sustaining authentic organizational change through shared purpose and culture.* Valencia College. Retrieved from http://valenciacollege.edu/trustee-education/documents/big-ideas-trustees.pdf

Simon, S. (2014, September 27). Maryland school shreds the old rules of applying to college [Interview]. (2014). Retrieved from http://www.npr.org/2014/09/27/351979016/maryland-school-shreds-the-old-rules-of-applying-to-college?utm_medium=RSS&utm_campaign=storiesfromnpr

Slaughter, S., & Leslie, L. (1997). *Academic capitalism: Politics, policies, and the entrepreneurial university.* Baltimore, MD: Johns Hopkins University Press.

Slaughter, S., & Rhoades, G. (2009). *Academic capitalism and the new economy: Markets, state, and higher education.* Baltimore, MD: Johns Hopkins University Press.

Smith, M. K. (2003). *Communities of practice.* Valencia College: infed. Retrieved from http://valenciacollege.edu/faculty/development/tla/documents/CommunityofPractice.pdf

Sternberg, R. J. (2003). *Wisdom, intelligence, and creativity synthesized*. Cambridge: Cambridge University Press.

Tagg, J. (2012, January-February). Why does the faculty resist change? *Change: The Magazine of Higher Learning*. Retrieved from http://www.changemag.org/Archives/Back%20Issues/2012/January-February%202012/facultychange-full.html

Thelin, J. (2011). *A history of American higher education*. Baltimore, MD: Johns Hopkins University Press.

Tinto, V. (1975). Dropout from higher education: A theoretical synthesis of recent research. *Review of Higher Education, 45*, 1, 89–125.

Tinto, V. (1986). Theories of student departure revisited. In John C. Smart (Ed.), *Higher education: Handbook of theory and research* (2, pp. 359–384). New York, NY: Agathon Press.

Tinto, V. (1988). Stages of student departure: Reflections in the longitudinal character of student leaving. *Journal of Higher Education, 59*(4), 438–455.

U.S. Census Bureau. (2014). Educational attainment in the United States: 2014 – Detailed tables. Washington, DC: Author. Retrieved from http://www.census.gov/hhes/socdemo/education/data/cps/2014/tables.html

University Innovation Alliance. (n.d.). The University Innovation Alliance to enhance access and success at public research universities: Vision and prospectus. Retrieved from http://www.theuia.org/sites/default/files/UIA-Vision-Prospectus.pdf

University of Maryland, Baltimore County. (n.d.a). *Breaking-Ground*. UMBC BreakingGround at Wordpress. Retrieved from https://umbcbreakingground.wordpress.com/

University of Maryland, Baltimore County. (n.d.b). *Freeman A. Hrabowski, III*. Retrieved from http://president.umbc.edu/

University of Wisconsin-Whitewater. (2015). *Liberal education and America's promise*. Retrieved from http://www.uww.edu/leap

Valencia College. (2014). *Faculty development catalog 2014–2015*. Orlando: Author. Retrieved from http://issuu.com/valenciacollege/docs/faculty_development-catalog_2014–15

Valencia College. (2015a). *Employment opportunities*. Retrieved from https://valenciacollege.csod.com/ats/careersite/search.aspx?site=1&c=valenciacollege

Valencia College. (2015b). *Faculty development*. Retrieved from http://valenciacollege.edu/faculty/development/

Valencia College. (2015c). *Human resources & diversity*. Retrieved from http://valenciacollege.edu/hr/

Volk, C., Slaughter, S., & Thomas, S. (2001, July/August). Models of institutional resource allocation: Mission, market, and gender. *The Journal of Higher Education, 72*(4), 387–413. Retrieved from http://www.jstor.org/stable/2672889

Wagner, T. (2010). *The global achievement gap: Why even our best schools don't teach the new survival skills our children need—and what we can do about it*. New York, NY: Basic Books.

Weidman, J. C. (1984). The school-to-work transition for high school dropouts. *Urban Review, 16,* 25–42.

Weidman, J. C. (1987). Undergraduate socialization. Paper presented at the Annual Meeting of the Association for the Study of Higher Education. ERIC Document Reproduction Services No. ED 292392.

Weidman, J. C. (1989). Undergraduate socialization: A conceptual approach. In John C. Smart (Ed.), *Higher education: Handbook of theory and research* (Vol. 5, pp. 289–322). New York, NY: Agathon Press.

Witham, K., Malcom-Piqueux, L. E., Dowd, A. C., & Bensimon, E. M. (2015). *America's unmet promise: The imperative for equity in higher education.* Washington, DC: Association of American Colleges and Universities.

Wood, D. J., and Gray, B. (1991). Toward a comprehensive theory of collaboration. *Journal of Applied Behavioral Science, 27,* 139.

INDEX